# THE DIVINE PROJECT

JOSEPH CARDINAL RATZINGER
(BENEDICT XVI)

# The Divine Project

*Reflections on Creation and Church*

EDITED BY
Michael Langer
Karl-Heinz Kronawetter

TRANSLATED BY
Chase Faucheux

IGNATIUS PRESS     SAN FRANCISCO

Original German edition:
*Gottes Projekt. Nachdenken über Schöpfung und Kirche*
© 2009 Verlag Friedrich Pustet, Regensburg
© Libreria Editrice Vaticana
English edition published by arrangement
with Eulama Literary Agency

Cover art:
*Expulsion from Paradise* (fresco detail)
Gurk Cathedral, Austria
© A. Dagli Orti /NPL-DeA Picture Library
Bridgeman Images

Cover design by Roxanne Mei Lum

© 2022 by Ignatius Press, San Francisco
All rights reserved
ISBN 978-1-62164-505-4 (PB)
ISBN 978-1-64229-234-3 (eBook)
Library of Congress Control Number 2022941281
Printed in the United States of America ∞

*To Georg Ratzinger on
his eighty-fifth birthday*

# Contents

# Foreword

The following book contains six lectures delivered in 1985 by Joseph Cardinal Ratzinger, then prefect of the Congregation for the Doctrine of the Faith, presented in their original form. These Carinthian lectures—held in the Austrian state of Carinthia at the bishop's formation house at Saint George's Abbey, Längsee—were part of an annual program where a theologian or a philosopher of the highest rank would be invited to give a series of lectures. Continuing until 2008 and involving participants from a number of different countries, the event had opened the previous year with Hans Urs von Balthasar as its first featured speaker. At that time, I was bishop of Carinthia, and von Balthasar gladly accepted my invitation; he had spoken there in front of several hundred students many times during my previous assignment as student chaplain at the universities in Graz. The series continued the following year with Cardinal Ratzinger, who agreed to come despite his extremely busy schedule. He did so in part due to his closeness to von Balthasar, but also because, as he told me in our first telephone conversation about the planned event, he believed that the topic of creation had fallen into theological obscurity, and he saw it as very important to bring it back out into the light before a large and intellectually very astute audience that would also include many young people.

Creation and redemption, these two themes that are deeply symphonic in their relation to one another, come up again and again in the work of Joseph Ratzinger, the professor and

9

the cardinal, who discusses them in a way that connects faith with beauty. Ratzinger repeatedly notes how indispensable it is to speak about God as Creator, particularly as we live in a society that increasingly denies the category of creatureliness, thus undermining man as man. This conviction continues to appear woven throughout the work of Joseph Ratzinger, Benedict XVI, today: God, in his love, created man and "stooped down" into history. It is in creation and salvation history that the Divine Word, through which all has come to be and through which man is created in the image of God, acts. The meaning of Christian existence is to recognize this by way of a reason that is open to God and to allow it to unfold in one's own life in the community of the Church by living a life of faith in the Word of God made fully manifest in the life, death, and Resurrection of Jesus Christ.

In August 2008, at a meeting with local priests and seminarians at Brixen Cathedral in South Tyrol, Benedict XVI said, his words crystal clear:

> Creation . . . awaits human beings who will preserve it in accordance with God. The brutal consumption of creation begins where God is not, where matter is henceforth only material for us, where we ourselves are the ultimate demand, where the whole is merely our property and we consume it for ourselves alone. And the wasting of creation begins when we no longer recognize any need superior to our own, but see only ourselves. It begins when there is no longer any concept of life beyond death, where in this life we must grab hold of everything and possess life as intensely as possible, where we must possess all that is possible to possess.[1]

[1] English translation from https://www.vatican.va/content/benedict-xvi/en/speeches/2008/august/documents/hf_ben-xvi_spe_20080806_clero-bressanone.html

The lectures given by Joseph Cardinal Ratzinger at Sankt Georgen more than twenty years ago are no less relevant today than they were then. Twenty-five years after the establishment of this distinguished summer forum, which was able to attract several other outstanding speakers, this model in its original form has come to an end. A special commemorative anthology featuring one text from each of these twenty-five summer discourses has recently been published by Friedrich Pustet Publishers, titled *Von Gott und der Welt*. I am happy to say that the Holy Father Pope Benedict XVI has agreed to allow his 1985 lectures at Saint George, Längsee, to be published here in this volume, also under the auspices of Friedrich Pustet. As then-bishop of Carinthia and his host on that occasion, and also on behalf of those who I am certain will find great joy and spiritual benefit in reading this book, I would like to express to him my own heartfelt gratitude.

Graz, October 7, 2008       +Egon Kapellari
Bishop of Graz-Seckau

# Preface

In the fall of 2008 we released a theology reader from the same publisher titled *Von Gott und der Welt*, which documented the Sankt Georgen Discourses and collected their contents in condensed form. The creation of this book required extensive research and a good bit of luck, until we at last came upon audio tape recordings of the lectures given by then-Cardinal-Prefect Joseph Ratzinger in September 1985 at Saint George's Abbey. It was like finding treasure in the attic. After the tapes were transcribed, both editor and publisher immediately decided not only to select one text for the collection, but also to publish all six of the lectures delivered on that occasion by Pope Benedict in a separate volume.

It therefore pleases us greatly that these precious texts are now being made accessible to the public. The print version of the lectures largely maintains their original, spoken form, leaving out citations and additional references.

We would like to thank Diocesan Bishop Dr. Egon Kapellari, who invited Cardinal Ratzinger to speak, for his introductory remarks and for obtaining permission from the Apostolic See to print this book. Apostolic protonotary Dr. Georg Schmuttermayr helped us out tremendously during the final editing process and provided us with valuable insights. Our employees Brigitte Cech and Maria Simon helped with the transcription of the tapes, and, as usual, Dr. Rudolf Zwank at Pustet did the proofreading. To all of them, a heartfelt *Vergelt's Gott*, as we say in Bavaria.

The cover of this small volume is adorned with an image from the fresco cycle in the bishop's chapel at Gurk Cathedral in Carinthia, Austria, a most impressive testimony to the thirteenth-century Romanesque period and largely preserved in its original colors. The detail in question depicts the introduction of Adam to Paradise: God and man stand facing one another, almost floating. In the middle is the Tree of Life and of Knowledge, framed by symmetrically positioned leaf and plant motifs. God blesses the archetypal man, who stands ready to receive the blessing with his left hand on his heart and his open right hand pointing toward his Creator. A banner describes what is happening: "Faciam(us) homine(m) ad imagine(m) et similitudine(m) no(stra)m"— "Let us make man in our image, after our likeness" (Gen 1:26).

Gurk Cathedral is a half hour by car from Sankt Georgen am Längsee. Knowing that Pope Benedict himself has on several occasions gazed on the marvelous frescoes in the bishop's chapel and prayed at the tomb of Saint Hemma makes us all the more pleased with this choice of cover design.

The publication of this compact volume [in German] coincides with the eighty-fifth birthday of the Holy Father's brother, Dr. Georg Ratzinger, apostolic protonotary and director emeritus of the Regensburg cathedral choir. We would like to take this occasion to wish him a very happy birthday and God's blessings for many years to come.

Oberaudorf/Regensburg    Michael Langer
Klagenfurt, Fall 2008    Karl-Heinz Kronawetter

# "In the Beginning, God Created . . ."

Our first concern in this opening lecture is to work out the standards that we will be using to interpret Scripture: How, indeed, can we properly understand a biblical text—not coming up with ideas of our own, but remaining honest with ourselves as interpreters of history—and yet, without doing violence to the text, inquire into its relevance for the present? This will then be followed by an attempt to ascertain the basic elements of what remains once we have worked out these standards. Then our third lecture should cover the topic of man's creation, with the fourth focusing on sin and the Fall, which of course, like all of God's judgments, are directed toward our salvation—a salvation he pursues even in his judgments.

Now before I begin, please allow me to read at least the first few lines of the text so that it is to some extent fresh in everyone's mind. After all, if we are going to interpret a text, it is best to have it in front of us, at least in some sense. And since it is one with which we are all familiar, I really only need to set the tone, so to speak:

> In the beginning God created the heavens and the earth. The earth was without form and void, and darkness was upon the face of the deep; and the Spirit of God was moving over the face of the waters.
>
> And God said, "Let there be light"; and there was light. And God saw that the light was good; and God separated the light from the darkness. God called the light Day, and

the darkness he called Night. And there was evening and there was morning, one day.

And God said, "Let there be a firmament in the midst of the waters, and let it separate the waters from the waters." And God made the firmament and separated the waters which were under the firmament from the waters which were above the firmament. And it was so. And God called the firmament Heaven. And there was evening and there was morning, a second day. (Gen 1:1–8)

We know how it goes from there: over the course of seven days, one element after another, then living things, then finally, on the sixth day, man is created, and, on the seventh day, God rests.

Hearing this passage again, though, there are two things that immediately stand out: On the one hand, there is the moving grandeur of the text, which to me sounds like a great, old church bell, possessing something of that primordial beauty that exceeds the bounds of ordinary discourse; on the other hand, though, there is also the tremendous strangeness of this text, transported to our own era and placed alongside our irrevocable knowledge of the processes by which the world came to be.

## Image and Truth

This raises the question: Is this merely a beautiful passage, or does this beauty also reveal something of the truth? And if so, how do we find it? This is a question people have been asking since the beginning—since the beginning of Christianity, as it were, and even earlier than that, since by the time this text entered the Greek and Latin-speaking world of

the Mediterranean—entered into the Christian world, that
is—it was already, from a scientific point of view, more or
less outdated. It embodied a different way of viewing and
understanding the world from the one that was common
and accepted. Things were somewhat different in the Middle Ages, but with the coming of the Modern Era, the question immediately returned to the fore, this time taking on
a growing sense of urgency.

I will get back to the question of how the ancient Church
dealt with this dichotomy between science and sacred text
later; for now, though, I am going to stay right here in the
present.

Indeed, after the Enlightenment, or let us say even after Galileo, it was an astonishingly long time before theologians really began to grapple with the question of how
the Christian, in the midst of this opposition between two
spiritual and intellectual realms that really should be one
and the same to him, can be both intellectually honest and
genuinely faithful. Leaving aside some earlier attempts for
now, a clear answer to the question was developed in the
interwar years by the likes of such names as Schmaus and
Guardini. It was the answer that I heard when I began to
study theology at the university in the first few years after
the Second World War, and one with which most of you are
probably somewhat familiar. It is one that I think does go
a long way toward answering the question, but it still does
not explain everything. But I am recalling it now because it
is a step we need to take before we can go any farther.

The answer, which gradually became the common point
of view in the field of Catholic theology starting in the
1930s, is based on the idea of literary genre. This view says
that the Bible is not a science textbook, nor does it claim

to be; it is a religious book, which means it cannot be used to acquire scientific information or to learn about how the world came to be as far as the natural processes involved are concerned. The only kind of knowledge that can be gained from it is religious knowledge; everything else is imagery, a way of making deeper, true realities accessible to man. And so, it was said, one has to distinguish between the form of presentation and the content being presented. The form is to be discerned based on the limits of people's understanding at the time, in the images in which they were immersed, in those with which they spoke and thought, through which they were able to intuit something greater, something real. And only this reality, that which shines forth through the images, is truly enduring. According to this view, Scripture is not trying to tell us how the different kinds of plants came about, how the sun and the moon and the stars were formed, but is ultimately using this imagery to say only one thing: that God created the world. The world is not, as many people in those days thought, a confused jumble of forces in conflict with one another, nor is it an abode of demonic powers against which man needs to protect himself. The sun and the moon are not deities that rule over us, and the heavens above us are not populated by hidden deities at war with one another. Rather, all of these things have their origin in a single power, God's eternal Reason, experienced in the creative power of the Word.

I do think it is worth noting what is being claimed here, because even if we all believe that polytheism is something that has been utterly overcome, our first experience of the world, even today, is essentially a polytheistic one. For anyone who looks at the world and experiences it—and even, I would say, accepts insights from the theory of evolution

as part of his life—perceives, on the one hand, the great,
the beautiful, the light, and the dark. But at the same time,
he also perceives—think of Reinhold Schneider's *Winter in
Wien*—the demonic, the uncanny, the negative in the world;
forces in opposition to one another, that is. The immediate
experience that we have of the world is not the monotheis-
tic experience, but a polytheistic one; we see that there are
forces and counterforces, powers in conflict with one another, some of which we need to protect ourselves against,
others on which we can rely for help. Into this original experience, which we can see did not just come about incidentally because people lacked enlightenment, but represents
the actual experience of man in every age, we see the introduction of this idea—an almost unreasonable one, really—
through the images of experiences that are transformed. It
is not a confusing jumble of powers standing in opposition
to one another; rather, there is only One, from whose will
all these things come, and that will is a good will.

Of course, this then brings up, in a different way, the task
of explaining the polytheistic reality, so to speak, that then
happens in Genesis 3, which we will get to later. But as far
as the present account is concerned, all that needs to be said
for the time being is that this all comes from the Word of
God, from the same God whom we encounter in the event
of faith.

Hence, the knowledge that the world has its origin in
the Word not only liberated man from the fear of gods and
demons, but also made the world free for reason to rise up
to God and opened the way for man to encounter this God
without fear. In this God, he experienced the true enlightenment that casts aside the gods and the occult forces and
allows him to recognize that there is ultimately only one

power behind all things, and we are in its hands. The living God is the same power that created this earth and the stars, the same power that sustains this entire universe. In this Word, we come into contact with the actual primordial force of the cosmos, with the actual power that is above all powers.

So far we have briefly outlined the view that was developed in the first half of the twentieth century: the distinction between the form in which the text is presented and its content, where the form is made up of images that do not really matter in and of themselves but that serve as the transparency, as it were, that allows us to see what is truly real. And thus, contrary to our initial impression of the text as a, shall we say, mythic account, this is the definitive breakthrough of real enlightenment in the world, the overcoming of fear, clearing the way for reason.

I think this view—the essential element of which is, I repeat once more, the distinction between the form in which a text is presented and the content it presents—is correct. Nevertheless, even when I heard it during my first year at university, I felt that there was something insufficient about it. See, when we are told that we need to distinguish between the images used and the meaning of the text, it seems liberating at first, but on second thought, you start to wonder: Why did no one say this before? I mean, they must have taught these things differently in the past, or else things like the trial of Galileo could not have happened. One begins to suspect that perhaps this view is ultimately nothing more than a trick used by the Church and the theologians, who are all out of ideas but do not want to admit it, so they are throwing up cover to dig in and hide behind. And generally speaking, all of these artful interpretive techniques—and I mean no disparagement by that—with which we are confronted on a daily basis, and are not limited to these texts, leave one with the impression that the history of Christianity over the past four hundred years has been one long rearguard action, in which, piece by piece, the claims of the faith and of theology are taken away from us, and we keep figuring out new ways of expressing things to allow us to make our retreat. But stepping back and taking full view of the path that we are on, one cannot help but fear that we are being slowly pushed out into the void and that the moment will come where there is nothing more to defend and nothing left to hide behind, where the entire territory of Scripture and faith will be occupied by a reason that will no longer permit any of this to be taken seriously. This is the moment of which Auguste Comte, one of the founders of positivism, was thinking when he said that in the end, all things would be in the domain of positive science. Anthropology, of course, resists this the hardest, since man is the most complicated of machines, but give it time and it will all be figured out eventually, and there will be nowhere else for theology to retreat.

Along with the sense of apprehension that anyone observing the theology scene over the past four hundred years will feel comes yet another disquieting thought—or perhaps it is really just a variation of the same thing. That is, one may begin to wonder: If theologians or even the Church can shift the boundaries between image and intended message like they do in this passage, between what would keep us stuck in the past and what is actually of consequence, then why not do so in other areas as well? What about the miracles of Jesus? Well, that has been done, too. And if it can be done there, what about the very heart of it all, the

Cross and Resurrection of Our Lord? It is an operation that attempts to defend the faith by admitting that we can no longer defend what is written in the text, but promising that there is an even truer reality behind it. More often than not, this kind of operation often ends up putting faith itself in doubt, since it raises questions about the honesty of the interpreter and whether there is anything at all that is unchangeable. Theological views of this sort have left quite a few people with the impression that the faith of the Church is like some kind of jellyfish, where there is nothing solid to grab onto, nothing firm at the center of it all that can be built upon.

Well-meaning though they are, these numerous half-hearted interpretations of the biblical Word are not capable of salvaging Christianity today, and to the ordinary listener they sound more like an evasion than an interpretation. Indeed, what they lead to is a sickly Christianity that does not really believe in itself and is thus unable to exude courage and enthusiasm. At times it comes across more like a social organization that just keeps on talking and doing things because it cannot do otherwise, though we all know there has not been anything left to talk about for some time.

And so we need to ask once more: Is this distinction between the image and the intended message just an evasion tactic we are using because we still want to make something of the text even though we can no longer stand behind it, or are there criteria from the Bible itself that lead us to do this; that is, does the Bible itself attest to this distinction? Does it give us any indications of this sort? And this brings us to the second question: Was the faith of the Church aware of these indications in the past as well? I believe that it is only when we can answer the first two questions that the importance of the other one becomes clear. So, first of all, what is the text itself actually telling us? And then, was this approach known to the Church in the past?

## The Unity of Scripture

So with these questions in mind, let us look at the text again. And when we do, the first thing we will notice is that Genesis 1, the text from which I just quoted a few verses, is, from its very beginning, not like some isolated boulder that is just standing there unconnected to anything else—indeed, Sacred Scripture in general was not written from beginning to end like a novel or a textbook; it is rather the echo of the history between God and his people that gradually coalesced into a single story. It arose from the paths taken by that history, from the struggles it involved, and through it we are able to catch a glimpse of the rises and falls, the sufferings and hopes, the glories and the failures of this history.

The Bible is thus an expression of God's long struggle with man to make himself understood to him. But at the same time, it is also an expression of man's long struggle to understand God. And just as the book as a whole grew through various historical situations of struggle that were then arranged into the structure we know, the matter of creation is not set down in one place, but accompanies Israel through its history, growing and developing in a continuous struggle. The entire Old Testament is a journeying with the Word of God, and the same goes for this particular theme. It was only in this journeying, where things might unfold, then become obscured again, that the message of the Bible was formed, text by text. And so it is not a collection of philosophical propositions or a series of questions and answers like a catechism, but a journey of understanding that develops and struggles. And because this is what it is, and no one text is complete and definitive but is always one stage in a struggle that has earlier stages and continues on afterward, we can only grasp the intended meaning of the individual text by looking at it in the context of the entire path and by understanding its inner progress, its inner direction.

Now this does not just apply to the part of Sacred Scripture that we call the Old Testament; rather, if we are viewing Scripture as a path, then the Old and the New Testaments need to be seen as part of the same whole. This is something that I think is very important for us as Christians. Today, as in every age, we are tempted by two opposing tendencies: We can reject the Old Testament and concede that it bears no intelligible relationship to what we, as Christians, believe—in other words, we can try to have a New Testament without an Old. Or, by the same token, we can view the New Testament as too spiritualistic and try to have the Old Testament only, as the more concrete and practical of the two. It is only when we see that the Bible is one path that we can understand that the New Testament, though much of what it says is indeed quite new, is part of the entire journey and, thus, needs to be interpreted with a unified understanding of the Old and the New Covenant.

For Christians, the Old Testament, taken as a whole, represents a journey toward Christ. Only when it arrives at Christ are we able to see what its true meaning, gradually hinted at, really was. Accordingly, each individual part derives its meaning from the whole, and the whole derives its meaning from its end, from Christ. So in order to interpret the text correctly in the theological sense—and this is something recognized by the Church Fathers and by the faith of the Church in every age—we cannot explore it in isolation, but, rather, we must understand it as part of a path that is leading us ever forward; we must understand that the true hermeneutic is to seek and to find its trajectory, the inner orientation of the path it is following.

This was a preliminary consideration that underpinned every interpretation of Scripture up to the time of the Renaissance: that the only way for someone to understand each individual text of Scripture is always to understand it as part of Scripture in its totality; and not like the totality of a textbook, either, but as a dynamic totality.

## Creation Beliefs in Israel and Surrounding Nations

Now, the question is, what is the significance of this insight when it comes to understanding our text, when it comes to understanding the story of creation? One of the first things we need to note is that Israel always believed in the Creator God, and it shared this belief with all of the great cultures of the ancient world. This observation was not always without controversy. Gerhard von Rad in particular, coming from the nineteenth-century exegetical tradition, presented a different vision, in which the salvation-historical creed first emerged as a purely soteriological creed, and then only gradually did the theme of creation emerge, developing around and expanding upon this soteriological creed.

It was Klaus Westermann, in his great commentary on Genesis, who demonstrated that this was not so, that in fact the theme of creation was present throughout the entire Oriental world and far beyond it, even in cultures that had no contact with one another at all, exhibiting the same basic structure, and that Israel, too, had always partaken of this basic idea. What is true—and we will get back to this later— is that this shared belief in creation only gradually coalesced into the specific form of faith in Yahweh. But the theme as such was always there, and, knowing this, we can break down the artificial barriers erected between the mythos and the faith of Israel, between the beliefs of the nations and those of the Bible, allowing us to see clearly once more the deep connections between the great cultures of mankind in their knowledge of this fundamental truth—a basic idea that was extraordinarily important to the Fathers and one that I believe acquires a new significance in the world's present situation in particular.

Even in those periods in which monotheism has been eclipsed, there has always been a knowledge of the Creator of heaven and earth, a fact that is demonstrated by a surprising degree of commonality between civilizations, including those that could never have been in actual contact with one another. And so I agree with Westermann that these commonalities allow us to glimpse something of the contact that man had with God's truth at the deepest level, a contact that was never entirely lost.

In Israel itself, the theme of creation passed through several different stages, and I would like to outline the main ones briefly. There are very few preexilic texts; one very ancient one is Genesis 14:18–22, the scene with Melchizedek, which goes: "And Melchizedek king of Salem brought out bread and wine; he was priest of God Most High. And he blessed him and said, 'Blessed be Abram by God Most High, maker of heaven and earth; and blessed be God Most High. . . .' And Abram gave him a tenth of everything. . . . But Abram said to the king of Sodom, 'I have sworn to the LORD God Most High, maker of heaven and earth.'"

So this is a very ancient, preexilic text that contains the phrase "maker of heaven and earth". The second preexilic text is Amos 5:8, which is a hymn of praise to Yahweh, of whom it says: "He who made the Pleiades and Orion, and turns deep darkness into the morning, and darkens the day into night, who calls for the waters of the sea, and pours them out upon the surface of the earth, the LORD is his name."

Then there are undoubtedly elements of the preexilic tradition contained in Genesis 1 itself, and the account in Genesis 2, the so-called Second Creation Account, is one that contains ancient creation beliefs. So what we have here are elements of and testimonies to preexilic beliefs about creation, even if they are sparse.

The second stage is then the exilic stage, where the idea really breaks through and is found in four major Old Testament Scripture complexes, suddenly becoming a central theme in Isaiah, Ezekiel, Deutero-Isaiah, and the so-called "Priestly Text" (Genesis 1).

And finally, there is the third, postexilic stage, with entirely new variations on the theme in the creation psalms, then all of the wisdom literature, and in particular the Second Book of Maccabees, which, in the context of the theology of martyrdom, developed the belief in creation *ex nihilo*. And I think it is quite significant that it is right when martyrdom is at hand and the question of a God with the power to restore dramatically enters into existence that we are able to perceive fully the clear recognition of creation from nothing.

So as this brief survey shows, the theme of creation was never entirely absent, but it was not always given equal importance. There were times when Israel was so preoccupied with the sufferings or the hopes of its own history, so intensely focused on the here and now, that there was hardly any use in looking back at creation; indeed, they hardly could. The actual moment in which creation truly became a dominant theme was during the Exile. It was during this period that the Genesis account—based on very ancient traditions, to be sure—took on its present form. Israel had left its land behind; it had lost its temple. According to the mentality of the time, the loss of the temple in particular was an unfathomable prospect, for it meant that the God of Israel had indeed been vanquished—he was a god whose people, whose country, whose worshippers could be taken away from him. A god who could not protect his worshippers and the worship of himself was a weak, no-account god; he had abdicated his divinity. And so being driven out of their land and erased from the map of nations was an enormous trial for the faith of Israel: Has our God been defeated? What about our faith?

At that moment, the prophets turned a new page; they taught Israel that what they were now seeing for the first time was the true face of their God, who was not bound to that particular strip of land and never had been. They showed them how to reread the story in reverse: after all, God had promised this piece of land to Abraham before he ever settled there, when it was populated by other people entirely. He had been able to lead his people out of Egypt, in spite of Pharaoh's great power. He had been able to do both of these things because he was not the god of one country, like all other gods, but had power over heaven and earth. And for the same reason he was able to work the Exodus miracle back then, he could now bring about the new Exodus; that is, he could expel his unfaithful people into another country in order to bear witness to himself there.

And so it came to be understood that this God of Israel was not a god who was more or less like the other gods, but was the God who had all lands and all peoples at his command. This was because he himself had created the heavens and the earth, because they were his own. It was in Israel's exile and apparent defeat that awareness emerged of the God who holds all peoples and all of history in his hands, who sustains all things in existence because he is the Creator of everything.

Now, this faith had to find its own identity, particularly in the face of temptations from the apparently victorious religion of Babylon, which was expressed in ostentatious liturgies, such as the celebration of the New Year, in which the re-creation of the world was celebrated and consummated liturgically. If, up to that point, it had been sufficient to share in what were more or less the common beliefs about creation, those beliefs now had to be attributed entirely to Yahweh. The elements that made this New Year's liturgy like a creation liturgy—rather typical for New Year's liturgies, as the new year is, after all, the end of one world and a renewal of creation—were primarily determined by the Babylonian creation account *Enuma Elish*, which describes in its own way how the world came to be. It says that the world arose out of a struggle between opposing forces and that it acquired its actual form when Marduk, the god of light, appeared and split the body of the primordial dragon in two, and it was from these two halves that the heavens and the earth came to be. Together, both the firmament and the earth are the sundered corpse of the slain dragon, and from its blood Marduk is said to have created mankind.

Now these were not all just fantastic tales, but experiences in the form of images—images that depicted man's experience of the world; namely, that the world is actually the body of a dragon, and man has dragon's blood in him. There is something sinister lurking at the bottom of the world; deep inside of man lies something rebellious, something demonic, something evil. In this way of viewing things, only the representative of Marduk—the dictator, the king of Babylon—can suppress the demonic and keep the world in balance.

Such views, I think it is now quite clear, are not simply fairytales, but reflect actual experience. Just think of how often it seems, even to us, that the world is a dragon's lair or that man has dragon's blood running through his veins.

Israel would have been all too familiar with these distressing experiences, and these stories would have been utterly believable to them; yet in the face of all of this, the scriptural account says no, that is not how it was.

The entire story of these sinister powers is reduced to just a few words in Genesis 1: "The earth was without form and void." The Hebrew words used here, *tohu wa bohu*, contain an echo of the expressions used elsewhere to describe the dragon [Heb. *tehom*], the demonic power. Now all that remains is the void, against which God alone stands as the sole power. And in the face of all fear of these demonic powers, the believers of Israel are told that God alone, the eternal Reason who is eternal Love, created the world, and that it rests in his hands.

I think that it is only against this background, in this context, that we can begin to comprehend the struggle that underlies Genesis 1. The real drama in this passage arises from its basic vital function, its inherent propensity to cast aside all these convoluted myths and instead place Divine Reason, the Word of God, at the origin of the world. In interpreting the text, it is possible to demonstrate almost word for word that this is, in a manner of speaking, the real tension that it is trying to convey. Like when the sun and moon are described as lamps that God hangs in the heavens to mark the passage of time—to people back then, it must have seemed like an outrageous sacrilege to designate the great deities the sun and the moon as lamps for keeping track of time! Here we see the boldness, the sober-minded clarity of faith that, in its struggle with the pagan powers, brings out the light of truth by showing that the world is not a contest between demons, but that it arose from reason, from Divine Reason, and that it is founded on God's Word.

And so, especially when reading it in the context from which it originally emerged, this creation account can indeed be seen as the definitive "enlightenment" of history, the point at which man was able to break through the oppressive fears that had held him down. It signifies the opening up of the world to reason, the recognition of the reasonableness that characterizes it and the freedom it offers. Now this brings up another question that we still need to address, but let me at least get out ahead of it by adding that another way in which this account shows itself to be the true enlightenment is that it does not just set human reason adrift to figure things out on its own, but firmly grounds it on the primordial bedrock of God's creative Reason, keeping it grounded in truth and love, without which enlightenment comes off as a self-indulgent and ultimately foolhardy endeavor.

Let us take it a step farther. I have just attempted to position this text in its own historical context, as it were—that is, in the pagan environment in which it took shape, thus revealing to us Israel's struggle to find the right way to incorporate the theme of creation into its faith. This is also apparent—and indeed we already went into this in more detail when we catalogued how beliefs about creation took shape —in the fact that the classic creation account is not the only creation text found in Scripture. It is immediately followed by another one, composed earlier and using a different set of imagery. There are still others in the Psalms, and the struggle to clarify beliefs about creation continues after that. The wisdom literature, in the encounter with Hellenistic civilization, reworks the theme—this is that step farther I was talking about—without feeling bound to the older images, like the seven days and so forth.

That is to say that we can see how the Bible itself constantly readapts the images it uses as ways of thinking continue to develop; we see how the Bible itself transforms them over and over so that it might testify more profoundly to the one thing that has truly come through in God's Word —the message that he is Creator. In other words—and this is crucial, I think—the images used in the Bible itself are not static, and by reading the images as a whole, we are able to experience the "nondogmatic" character of the individual images, since they are not fixed and are continually being revised. And so, the attentive reader is able to see, via a gradual and ongoing process, that they are merely images that reveal something deeper and greater.

## The Theme of Creation throughout Scripture

So the first step is to understand things in their own context, that of interaction with the pagan world; the second one, to understand the Bible, the Old Testament process from within. After these comes the third step, which, as we already mentioned at the start of all this, is to understand that the Old Testament is not the end of the path. The matters contemplated in the so-called wisdom literature make up the final bridge on a long road, one that leads to the message of Jesus Christ, to the New Covenant. And only there do we find the ultimate, definitive creation account in Scripture, the one that provides Christians with the standard for interpreting every other creation text. This ultimate and definitive biblical creation account opens with the key verses: "In the beginning was the Word, and the Word was with God, and the Word was God. . . . All things were made through him, and without him was not anything made that was made" (Jn 1:1, 3).

It is obvious that John is quite deliberately echoing Genesis 1 here. In exegesis, you hear about the "inner relecture" of the Bible, meaning that the Bible rereads its own experiences with each passing generation, thus interpreting them itself. The Evangelist was consciously hearkening back to the opening words of the Bible, rereading the creation account with Christ in mind to remind us once more of the Word behind the images, the Word by which God desires to jolt our hearts.

Now earlier I said that a basic axiom of proper Scripture interpretation, one recognized by the Early Church, was that interpreting Scripture in the theological sense means reading it in its entirety and in view of its overall trajectory. And this brings us to the Church Fathers' second fundamental hermeneutical principle, namely, that contained within this overall picture—which is to be read in terms of its general direction—is what we might call a privileged key: the New Testament. We do not read the Old Testament by itself and for its own sake, but always with the New Testament and through the New Testament.

This is why even though we are no longer obliged to follow the Law of Moses, the purification rituals, the dietary laws, and all those other things, the biblical Word is not thereby rendered meaningless and insignificant. We still read it as the Bible and as the Word of God, even today. As Christians, we claim that our reading of it is the correct one, but at the same time can only really claim to be reading it correctly when we read it with Christ; and even then, by penetrating beyond a certain kind of literalness— not away from the Word, but right into the heart of the Word. And this, as the Fathers never tire of pointing out, does not just apply to a handful of passages, like the dietary laws, for instance—rather, it applies to the Old Testament as a whole. We do not read it as something that is complete and sufficient unto itself; we read it with him in whom all things are fulfilled and in whom the ultimate, actual validity and truth it contains are thus revealed.

And so when we read the Law and even the creation account, which is part of the Law, we read it with Christ, and it is from him—from him, you see, not from some gimmick that we came up with after the fact—that we know what God wished to convey to the human heart and soul gradually over the centuries. Christ, as the Fathers tell us precisely with regard to such passages, has freed us from bondage to the letter, and in the same way he restores for us the truth of the images.

To the Church of Antiquity and the Middle Ages, this was self-evident, and they saw it as the fundamental guiding principle of their own efforts to live according to the Word of God. They understood that the Bible is one whole and that we can only truly hear what it is saying if we hear it as coming from Christ. This means hearing it in the freedom that he has given us and from the depths where, through the screen of images, he reveals the true and enduring reality, the solid ground on which we can always stand.

It was only at the dawn of the modern era that people began gradually to forget this dynamic of the living unity of Scripture that can only ever understand with Christ, in the freedom that he gives us and in the certitude that comes from this freedom.

Parallel to the rise of the scientific way of thinking came the rise of a historical way of thinking that attempted to apply to texts and to history more or less the same methods used by the natural sciences on nature. Thus, in accord with its scientific idealism, this emerging form of historical thinking now sought to read each text in isolation, purely in terms of its historically literal meaning. Using purely historical methods, there is nothing in an individual text to suggest it should be read in the context of the Bible as a whole, since after all, Jeremiah and Amos were writing in entirely different periods, the wisdom literature and Ezekiel were written by entirely different authors, and so on. The integrity of the Bible as such is a matter of faith, which has its place and its empirical justification in the way that it roots the path of the people of God. As a purely historical matter apart from this life context, it is not a matter of historical reality, but as nineteenth-century exegesis had it (and which, objectively speaking, is correct in a purely historical sense): it is an extremely heterogeneous collection of literature gathered under a single book cover.

Thus, people now only sought to explain the exact meaning of the individual text, forgetting all about the Bible as a unified whole. To put it another way, people were no longer reading it forward—as a coherent, living world of struggle and understanding despite the authors coming from various generations—but backward, as defined by the methodology. This meant always looking for the more ancient source, the true origin, the oldest stage of development, and permitting this alone to be considered valid content for interpretation. The texts were no longer read forward, but backward—not with a view to Christ, but back toward the presumed origin of the text.

No longer did one look to the ultimate form to discern

the meaning of a text or the nature of a thing; but one looked
to the beginning, to its origin. The Fathers' way of reading
in view of Scripture as a totality came to be disparaged as
"allegory". And because reading in light of the totality of
Scripture was mere "allegory", and thus the very antithesis
of the scientific approach, this approach soon just vanished
from theology as a scholarly discipline. The right approach
would have been a different one, namely, to get past those
elements that we may rightly call "allegory" in a derogatory
sense, in order to discover all the more the genuine language
of the unity of the one Bible. The task, it seems to me, that
is now given to our generation is the great mission of a new
phase in the history of exegesis. This way of isolating the
text from the whole, that is, this literal-mindedness with respect of particulars that contradicts the entire inner nature of
the biblical texts, but which is now regarded as the only real
scholarly approach—and which has of course provided us
with valuable insights—is what led to the conflict between
the natural sciences and theology that has been, up to our
own day, a serious burden on faith.

## Creation and Reason

This does not have to be the case, because from the beginning, faith has always been greater, broader, and deeper.
There is nothing unrealistic about believing in creation, even
today. Even when we look at the findings of the natural sciences, it is the better hypothesis, offering a fuller and better explanation than all other theories. Faith is reasonable.
The reasonableness that exists in creation is derived from
Divine Reason; there is no other truly convincing explanation for it. What Aristotle said four hundred years before

Christ against those who claimed that everything came into being by chance [*ek thaumatos*] still holds true today—and he thought of this even without the belief we have in creation. The reasonableness of the world enables us to recognize the Reason of God, and the Bible is and continues to be the true enlightenment that has given the world over to human reason—and not to exploitation by human beings, because it (reason, that is) opens the way to God's truth and God's love. And thus in our own day, there is no need for us to hide our belief in creation or the creation texts of the Bible. We *must* not hide them, because only if it is true that the universe is the result of freedom, of love and reason, only if these are the real underlying forces at play, can we trust one another, can we enter into the future together, can we speak as human beings. It is only because God is the Creator of all things that he is Lord of all things, and it is only because of this that we can pray to him. For this means that freedom and love are not powerless ideas, but that, despite all appearances, they are the fundamental powers of reality.

# Creation and Reason

In setting out to establish some standards for interpreting the creation account, and for a theological approach to interpreting Scripture in general, we have come up with two in particular: first, that Scripture is to be read as a path, in its full totality, and second, more precisely, that the Old Testament and the New Testament both light the way for each other along the totality of this path. And what this means in concrete terms for us as Christians is that we read Scripture with Christ. He is our guide through it all, and we can count on him to show us what is image, and where the true, enduring content of a biblical passage may be found.

He is at the same time, we said, our liberation from a false bondage to literalism and our guarantee of finding the best, the realistic, and not arbitrarily interchangeable truth of the Bible, the truth that does not dissipate in a fog of pious pleasantries but remains the firm ground on which we stand.

To the first, more structural of these findings—though it tells us quite a bit about God's action throughout all of history, and the accessibility, the comprehensibility, and the perceptibility of this action—we then added a concrete conclusion, which I, however, formulated more by way of anticipation: namely, that belief in creation, as we come to understand it by reading the Bible in its totality, is reasonable. While reason might not be able to arrive at this belief on its own, it still calls out for it and finds in it the response for which it was looking and which at the same time helps it to get its own insights in order and fit them into the whole.

Now I had planned to do two things with this lecture, but I am actually going to try and scale things back a bit. The first thing I wanted to do was to consider what we have learned or anticipated up until now and explore it in more detail. And the issue of man's creation would actually be included in this, because it is not really until this point that we are able to grasp the full gravity of the question of how faith and reason can be brought into relation with one another in belief in creation. And then, so it seems to me, there is a second point we ought to consider, that is, the question—one that has become so relevant today—of what is actually meant by that famous line "fill the earth and subdue it." In what manner have the Bible and, thus, Christianity incurred responsibility for the way in which we have handled the world, dealing with it in ways that are destructive to it?

But thinking about all this, I came to the conclusion that this would perhaps be a bit too much to fit into one lecture. So for now, I would like to set aside the question of man's creation—though it is a huge issue in its own right—and make do with some initial reflections on the question of the reasonableness of creation, which I will then have to follow up in another lecture with the question of man. But in asking about the reasonableness of creation, we are presented with the most basic example of what it means to say that "God acts" in light of the beginning, since if he did not act there, then he never acts, and, likewise, if he did act there, then we have a basic model of what we mean when we talk about God's action in history in general.

Because this question carries so much weight, I am going to content myself with just trying to approach it from a few different directions for now, and then I will attempt to present the second thing—which I do think is sufficiently important for our current situation in the world, for the kind of historical responsibility that we bear—in a bit more detail.

## Reason in Creation and the Reason of God

Let us begin, first of all, with the question of the reasonableness of creation. In the first lecture, we were largely content to say that this text (Gen 1) tells us *that* God created. This "that", of a contingent world in which nothing exists of itself and nothing can account for itself, requires that which *is* of itself in order to account for anything that is not of itself.

While this philosophical insight is in itself quite reasonable, by the nineteenth century, it was not seen as particularly evident at all, a view that appears to be shared by many today as well. In the nineteenth century, you see, the natural sciences were particularly informed by the two great laws of conservation, the law of conservation of matter and the law of conservation of energy. However, because of the considerable impact that the two laws of conservation had on the image that people had of nature and the world, the whole universe was presumed to be an ever-existing cosmos governed by the unchanging laws of nature, which ultimately necessitates no further hypotheses or questions, but exists of itself and in itself and has no need of anything outside of itself. It was simply there, in its entirety. This is what enabled Laplace to say that he no longer needed the hypothesis of God; that is, he said: "If we can just explain this and that, then we will not need God as a hypothesis anymore." But it seemed they were virtually there already.

But then new discoveries were made. One of these findings was the law of entropy, which states that energy, when consumed, is transformed into a different state and cannot be restored. This means that the world follows a course of coming to be and passing away, with temporality written into its very structure. After that came the discovery that matter can be transformed into energy, and based on these two discoveries, the laws of conservation were themselves modified. Finally came the theory of relativity, and many other discoveries, all of which, when taken together, showed that the world had its own built-in timepieces, so to speak, and from these "timepieces" we can see that there is a beginning and an end, a passage of time from beginning to end. Even if the time in question spans immeasurable distances and scientists come up with ever older dates, the knowledge that cosmic existence is fundamentally temporal in nature nevertheless allows us to discern once more, through the obscurity of billions of years, that moment which the Bible refers to as the beginning. And that beginning points to the one who had the power to set existence itself into being, to say "let there be" and there was. Or, to put it another way, we once again have to distinguish between what is *not* necessary, that which by its very nature comes into and passes out of existence, and what *is* necessary.

A second thing to consider is that the more we discover of the universe, the more we find a kind of reason in it all, whose ways we try to follow. Today there is even this idea from America that is gaining steam, the hypothesis that the universe is anthropically determined—that is, that even a tiny difference in the starting conditions of the universe would have meant that man could not exist. But as things did turn out, there does seem to have been a kind of determination at play in the course that the universe ultimately followed. But be that as it may, let us go ahead and leave that hypothesis alone for now. Everything that we are learning about, from the very smallest thing to the very largest, enables us to see things anew, and the scientific formulas, as it were, are an opportunity for us to reflect on the Creator Intelligence to which our own reason owes its existence.

I always like to refer here to the still-unsurpassed words of Albert Einstein, who once said that the laws of nature reveal "an intelligence of such superiority that, compared with it, all the systemic thinking and acting of human beings is an utterly insignificant reflection." Now it is well known that this did not lead Einstein to a concept of a personal God, and of course we are not dealing with a fully developed theology here. But what he says is nevertheless an expression of the principle that all of science rests upon, that human thought in its own meager way is able to contemplate a Reason that is forever immeasurably greater than ours, a Reason that preexists us and that also enables our own power of reason.

We are able to recognize in the immense objects that make up the world of the stars and other heavenly bodies a great and powerful Reason that holds the universe together. And as we penetrate ever deeper into the smallest of things, into the cell, into the primordial units of life, there, too, we discover a reasonableness that is truly astonishing, so that today I believe we can no longer say that Saint Bonaventure was merely being pious; rather, he was also being reasonable, when he said—very much in the tradition of the Wisdom Books, I might add—"Whoever does not see all this is blind. Whoever does not hear all this is deaf. And whoever does not begin to worship and praise the Creator Intelligence based on all this is dumb."

Allow me to relate another instance, one from what we

might call the "other side"; it is a bit of a funny story, but in my opinion it is also a powerful one. Jacques Monod, as is well known, categorically rejected any belief in God as unscientific, and in one impressive work he attributed the origin of the universe to the interplay between chance and necessity. But in this very book, which was translated from French and sums up his worldview, he relates how after attending the lectures that would ultimately form the basis for the book, François Mauriac is supposed to have said, "What this professor wants to inflict on us is far more unbelievable than what we poor Christians were ever expected to believe."

Monod himself says that Mauriac was actually right—that it really is even more unbelievable, but unfortunately, it happens to be scientifically true. Indeed, his thesis, which we are going to come back to in the next lecture, is that "the whole concert of animate nature"—that is exactly how he phrased it—"arose entirely from errors and dissonances, loud discordant tones, which miraculously come together in a concert." Thus, he himself admitted—and this honesty is what makes his work so impressive—that in itself such a notion is absurd; but, he insisted, the scientific method compels us to cast aside as unscientific any question that might lead in the direction of a creative Reason if there is no other way to answer it. This, I think, is where a certain definition of the scientific method is revealed to be unreasonable, and hence unscientific as well, inasmuch as science is presumably concerned with reason.

So in that regard, having seen the ramifications of this counter-experiment, as it were, we can now say, in light of everything we know, that when we observe the reasonableness of creation, what we see is God himself looking back at us. People like Manfred Eigen and others have attempted to show that random chance is reasonable, using game theory and such to explain away its very discordant nature. But I do not believe they have been able to change Monod's diagnosis in any fundamental way. In this respect, it can be said that physics and biology, the natural sciences in general, as long as they keep within their own domain of course, do not reveal the existence of God—indeed, such a God could only be a very diminished one. Yet in the very limits to what they are able to tell us, and by those things to which they implicitly point, they have in fact provided us with what I see as a new, heretofore unheard-of creation account, one with grand, new images in which we might recognize the face of the Creator, the God who acts, reminding us all over again that at the very beginning and foundation of all being stands the Creator Intelligence. The world is not the product of darkness and senselessness. It arises from intelligence, it arises from freedom, and it arises from a beauty that is love. And seeing this, amid all the horrors of the world, gives us courage to keep living and empowers us to embark confidently on the adventure of life.

So what I wanted to do with this was to develop this line of reasoning from our previous lecture a bit farther. We are still left with the ongoing task of trying to understand precisely what it means to say "God acts." To these reflections, I would now like to add one more step, as I have already mentioned. Thus far, I have tried to make it clear that the creation accounts in the Bible represent a different way of speaking about reality than the one we know from physics and biology. And this is how they were intended, not just something we say now that we know better. They do not depict the process by which things came to be or the mathematical structure of the world; rather, what they tell us, in various ways, is that there is only *one* God. The world is not

a battle between dark and shadowy forces but is rather the
creation of one God.

## The Truth behind the Images

But this then brings us to a question that has always concerned me, even as a university student: Is this all we are
left with from these chapters and from all the other creation
texts in Scripture? Are we not asking the images to do too
much of the work here? I would say, no, this is not all we
are left with. In any case, if we recognize that these texts
are primarily concerned with communicating this basic message, that does not mean that the individual passages of the
biblical text—that is, the various images we find in them—
now just sink into meaninglessness, leaving us, as it were,
with nothing but these new images, this bare extract. The
individual images express truth, too, even if they do not all
do so in the same way; but again this truth is different from
the kind of truth with which we are familiar from physics
and biology. They express truth in the manner of symbols,
much as a Gothic window is able to communicate incredibly
profound things with the effect of the light passing through
it and the signs and symbols that decorate it.

Now, I do want us to stay focused on a systematic approach to these issues and not get carried away with exegesis, so let me emphasize two key points here.

The first is that the biblical creation account is characterized by its use of numbers. These numbers, however, reflect
not the mathematical structure of the world but, rather, the
inner pattern that is woven into its fabric, so to speak—
the idea upon which it is built. Predominant among them

are the numbers three, four, seven, and ten; and for now I would like to focus on only two of these, seven and ten. The words "God said" appear ten times in the creation account. And since this is a very careful and deliberate account, we can say with certainty that this is no coincidence. Rather, by having God speak ten times in the creation account—ten words of God—the creation narrative already anticipates the Decalogue; that is, the Ten Commandments. In this way, it already points to the inner unity of God's singular action in creation and history, of his singular act of speaking, thus revealing to us, in the very pattern of creation, the God who speaks for history. It allows us to see that the "ten words" that we call the Ten Commandments are, as it were, nothing less than the echo of creation. They are not arbitrary inventions meant to put up barriers to human freedom, but signs pointing to the spirit, the language, the meaning of creation. They are thus a translation of the language of the universe, a translation of the logic of God, which this world anticipates. So that is the number ten, then. The Decalogue, the Ten Commandments, are simply a translation, so to speak, of the inner Word of creation itself and of the action that emanates from it, which is present within creation and does not override our own action.

The other number, the one that dominates the whole creation account, is seven. Indeed, the schema of the seven days makes it impossible to overlook how thoroughly the entire account is shaped by this number. Seven is the number of days in a lunar phase, and thus we are told throughout this account how the rhythm of our heavenly companion reveals to us the rhythm of human life as well. It becomes clear that we human beings are not trapped within our own little "I", but that we are part of the rhythm of the universe; that we too can learn from the heavens, as it were, the rhythm, the movement, of our own lives by attuning ourselves to the reason inherent in the universe.

I believe that this is something very important. Human existence is perpetually open to the cosmos; we are not entangled in the things of the earth, let alone our own affairs and the little bit of work that we do; rather, the whole universe is locked together in a rhythmic cycle from which we derive the rhythm of our own lives, and by taking our place in this rhythm we consummate the world as we ought.

But then the Bible takes this idea one step farther. It tells us that the rhythm of the heavenly bodies is, in a deeper sense, an expression of the rhythm of the Heart that created the heavens and mankind, an expression of the rhythm of God's love, which manifests itself in them.

## Creation Accounts and Cultic Worship

With that, we have now arrived at the next figurative element of the creation account that I wanted to discuss. For here we encounter not only the "rhythm of seven" and its cosmic significance, we also see how this rhythm itself serves to tell us something even deeper. Creation, as the account tells us via the rhythm of seven, is oriented toward the Sabbath, which is the sign of the covenant between God and mankind. And we can say that while the rhythm of seven does signify the things I have just indicated, the primary reason for which it was introduced was to present the Sabbath as the ultimate goal of creation. As such, we can now draw the initial conclusion that creation itself is structured in such a way that it is oriented to the hour of worship. Creation was done so that there would be a space for worship.

Creation is wholly fulfilled, serves its purpose, when it is a house of worship, so to speak, when it is lived with a view to worship. Creation exists for the sake of the Sabbath, it exists for the sake of the covenant, and it exists for the sake of worship. "Operi dei nihil præponatur", Saint Benedict says in his Rule: "Let nothing be preferred to the Work of God." This is not an expression of an excessive piety or an attempt to escape the world or anything like that, but a clear and sober rendering of the creation account, of the message that it bears for our lives. The true center, the power that moves and shapes from within in the rhythm of the stars and our lives, is worship.

So then, if the rhythm of the universe is governed by worship, it gives justification to life and to history, for it is at this central point that the action of God and the action of man come into contact with one another, thus setting the world aright. This again brings us to a remarkable matter to which I already alluded in my first lecture, namely, the way in which the world's peoples shared in this primordial knowledge. When it comes down to it, this knowledge is present in all cultures, even if it is often rather distorted, and the creation accounts in every culture in which they are found ultimately prove to offer a rationale for religious worship, or "cult", to say that the world exists for cult, for the glorification of God.

As many of you know, I came of age as a theologian during the era of Karl Barth, and my professors were also deeply influenced by him, so that more or less everything we thought and did as theologians revolved around the *distinctiveness* of the Christian faith, how different it was from other cultures and other religions. Now, the more time that I have had to study and practice theology, the more clearly I realize how wrong he was. The recognition of unity among

the world's cultures on the deepest questions of human existence is a crucially important development; indeed, it is
also the essential reason why there can be such a thing as
"inculturation" in the first place, since cultures are already
more or less in agreement with one another on this decisive
point and are consequently open to the idea. At every bishops' synod, whether in conversation with the bishops or in
the discussions in the plenary sessions, it is always a new
experience for me to see how much closer the great ancient
or, at any rate, old cultures are to the actual testimony of the
Bible and that of the Early Church than our modern way
of thinking.

So, when discussing matters of inculturation, if we take
our present constructs and extrapolate the kinds of fan-
ciful Christianities that might emerge from this process,
they mostly end up being reflections of the utopias that
we "Westerners" imagine. And then if we actually know a
culture, we ought to be able to say that, on the contrary, if
we enculturate ourselves in that culture, we will be led back
to a much more profound understanding of our origins, to
the basic witness of the Old and the New Testaments, and
the Church of the Fathers. I am thinking, for example, of
the discussions at the Synod on the Family, or the Synod
on Penance, where basically all cultures are familiar with
penitential rites and theologies that are much more similar
to those that characterized the Ancient Church than they
are to modern conceptions.

So there is this deep unity among cultures with respect to
the primordial knowledge of mankind that is open to Christ,
and that is why it is becoming increasingly clear to me that
the real debate might even be the other way around: The
danger confronting those of us who live in technological
civilizations is that we have cut ourselves off from this pri-

mordial knowledge, which has actually always been present and even now is still capable of holding things together. While it no longer says anything to us, who consider as certain only so-called scientific knowledge—the kind derived from developments in the technical sciences—we can no longer be sure of anything we get from primeval human beings. Our problem is that we misunderstand the nature of science, thinking we know better, and this essentially prevents us from hearing what creation is trying to teach us, and that we are actually—perhaps as a grace of our moment in history—given the task of inculturation as a guidepost back to that which truly sustains mankind and has connected us since the beginning.

So the first thing for us to say in reference to the concrete example is that creation accounts tend to provide a rationale for religious worship, meaning that the message they wish to convey is that the "why", the purpose, of creation is worship. We should now add, however, that this knowledge, which mankind once possessed and still does, always appears in a distorted form, though indeed in such a way that its true content, so to speak, still shines forth and is not simply lost. The major religions of the world are familiar with the grand idea that man exists for the purpose of worship, but this idea is then deformed by the belief that in the act of worship, man is giving to the gods something they need. It is thought that the deity needs human beings to provide this service and that, in this way, cult sustains the world. Cult, in this view, is the means by which the world is perpetuated: the cycle of the world is that the gods make man and the world, but that mankind exists to sustain the gods, and so the whole cycle is completed and continues to repeat itself forever. This idea of "do ut des"—where each one gives to the other because they need each other—

opens the door to speculation about power, and the thought of power corrupts the notion of love. And having twisted love into power, relationship into dependency, man can now tell himself: The gods need me, and that means I can put pressure on them, even extort them if I need to. Out of the pure relationship of love that worship was intended to be, there arises the manipulative attempt to seize control over the world and to shape it however we want by means of the power we have been given.

When this happens, cult degenerates into a distortion of both the world and of man. Now, the Bible is acquainted with the same fundamental notion that the universe exists for the sake of worship. It is safe to say that in a certain sense, the purpose of Genesis 1 itself is to provide a basis for cultic worship. I should probably add here, however, that this view was particularly opposed by Protestant theologians of the forties, fifties, and even the sixties, who claimed that the association of creation with cult worship was typical of paganism, and this position had a profound effect on us as well. The Old Testament is the antithesis of this idea, they would say; and if it culminates in the Sabbath and commands man to rest, but also previously commanded him to act, then the biblical account of worship culminates in socially conscious, world-shaping action. And according to this view, what makes Christianity and paganism antithetical to one another is that paganism is all about cultic worship, and Christianity is socially conscious and oriented toward shaping the world. And this of course ultimately resulted in the reduction of Christianity to the social, to the horizontal, among other things.

I do not believe this alternative view actually holds up with respect to the text. Here, too, the Sabbath is held to be the sign of the covenant, and here, too, it says that creation takes its structure from the order of the Sabbath, and the Sabbath is in turn the recapitulation of the Torah, the Law of Israel. This, however, is the added nuance, for it means that worship has a moral aspect to it. Incorporated into it is the entire moral order of God; only then is it truly worship.

And one more thing I should say here is that the Torah, as the law, is an expression of the history that Israel experienced with God. It is an expression of the covenant, but the covenant is an expression of the love of God, of his "yes" to man, whom he created both to love and to receive love.

This, however, allows us to grasp the idea presented in the Bible more precisely. We can say that God created the world in order to enter into a history of love with mankind. In its very essence, his creative action is the action of history, lasting consistency for the sake of the new world, unity that is love. He created it so that love might exist. Behind this observation we once again find the words of Israel pointing directly to the New Testament. In Jewish literature, it is said that the Torah, which embodies the mystery of the covenant and the history of the love between God and man, was there in the beginning. It was with God, and through it, all things that came to be came to be. It was the light and it was the life of mankind.

The author of the Gospel of John only needed to take these formulas and apply them to him who is the Living Word of God in order to say: "All things came into being through him" (Jn 1:3). The letter to the Colossians puts it this way: "All things were created through him and for him" (Col 1:16). God created the world in order to become a human being and to pour out his love and to bestow it on us and to draw us into union with himself. That makes this one more instance where the inner unity of the Old and New Covenant is made manifest precisely in the interaction between them.

## *"Let Nothing Come before Service to God"*

Now we need to go one step even farther and look for a way to understand this in greater depth. In the creation account, the Sabbath is depicted as the day on which man, in the freedom that is worship, participates in the freedom of God, in God's rest, and thus in God's peace. To celebrate the Sabbath is to celebrate the covenant. It requires us to return to the source, to clear away all the defilements brought about by our own work. And at the same time, it means moving forward into a new world where there will no longer be slaves and masters, but only free children of God; to a world in which man and beast and earth will, as family, share together in God's peace and God's freedom. For after all, that is what this depiction of the seventh day is telling us, that this is the day of shared participation by all creatures in the peace of God and that all are free brothers and sisters.

It is from this basic idea that the Mosaic social law developed. In this respect, then, it is quite correct to say that the social aspects of faith are contained right here in the creation account. The reason for this is that the Sabbath brings about universal equality. This is then expanded beyond the weekly Sabbath day, where one day stands in anticipation of a society free of domination, by establishing every seventh year as a Sabbath year, during which the earth and mankind may rest, prefiguring the new society. And then every seventh year times seven is the great Sabbath year, when all debts are canceled and all sales and purchases are annulled. Everyone starts over again, and in this new beginning the world is received anew from the hands of God the Creator, a true re-creation.

This order of things was probably always an ideal that was never realized as such, though nevertheless we might say that the fact that it is an ideal order is precisely what makes it so important from the point of view of theology. The high degree to which it was valued in the Old Testament is most apparent to me in a brief observation made in the Second Book of Chronicles. Now I already mentioned in the first lecture how the suffering experienced by the Israelites during the Exile included what we might call theological dimensions, in that God, as it were, denied himself, taking away the Israelites' land, their temple, and their means of worshipping him. But this is something they continued to reflect on even after the Exile. How could God do such a thing to them? Why this excessive punishment, to the point where it seemed that God was punishing himself? Of course, they could not have known then how he would, indeed, take all punishment on himself on the Cross, how he would allow himself to be wounded in his love affair with mankind, how he would show himself to be the one who acts in history precisely by appearing in it as one who suffers and, in suffering here, overcoming our wrongdoing.

And so, the question people asked was, "How could this be?" And as this was such a big question, there were of course many attempts to answer it. One answer that carries a good deal of weight comes at the end of the Second Book of Chronicles. What it says is that all of the many sins that the prophets stood up against, all the moral failure, all the things for which Israel certainly deserved criticism—in the end, none of it could be sufficient reason for such unfathomable punishment, for their land to be taken away from them for seventy years, leading to the closing of the temple for seventy years. The reason for this had to be something even deeper, something that was closer to the roots, something more radical. And I find that the answer given in Chronicles is one that is very much worth meditating on. In 2 Chronicles 36:21, it says: "The land had enjoyed its sabbaths. All the days that it lay desolate it kept sabbath, to fulfil seventy years." It was the Sabbath that people were unwilling to keep, and now they have got to make up for it. In other words—if we really try to get all the way to the bottom of this theological reflection—man saw his actions, his doings, his work, his self-possession, his self-realization, his belongings, as more important than the end for which creation existed, this goal of entering into freedom together, this fraternal coexistence within creation. He had refused God's rest, his gift of leisure, the worship of him and the peace and freedom associated with it. And so, because he wanted to be the sole agent in his life, acting alone and of his own accord, owing everything to his own freedom, he became ensnared in the tangled web of his own activity and his own control, falling into the bondage of action and dragging the world along with him.

He drove the world into the slavery of his activity, thereby enslaving himself as well. For this reason, God, in order to save him—remember again that judgment is not a punishment imposed on positivist grounds, but a means of inner healing—for this reason, God, in order to heal man of this very sin from within, had to give him the Sabbath that he no longer wanted for himself. In his "no" to the God-given rhythm of freedom and leisure, man had distanced himself from the image of God within himself and, in doing so, had also trampled on the world underfoot. For this reason, he had to be snatched away from his stubborn attachment to his own works, from his warped focus on himself, from seeing and wanting only himself. It is for this reason that God had to bring him back to his true self, to free him from the domination of activity. "Operi dei nihil præponatur"— I believe that this saying of Saint Benedict's, "Let nothing be preferred to the service of God," becomes fully relevant in this context as well: The priority of worship as the true end of creation, and therein man's freedom, and only within this order can human beings truly function as human beings.

## *"Fill the Earth and Subdue It"*

Now with this in mind, we come to the final consideration I wanted to address in this lecture, to which I actually briefly alluded at the beginning. There is one passage in the creation account that attracts only negative attention these days, and it requires special interpretation. I am referring to the famous verse Genesis 1:28, when God tells mankind to "fill the earth and subdue it."

Many have begun to use this sentence as a starting point for attacks against Christianity. The "merciless consequences" of this passage supposedly demonstrate that Christianity is self-refuting and is wholly responsible for the misery of our time. Indeed, the Club of Rome started with these ideas well over a decade ago [1972]. In rightly pointing out the limits of growth and the problems associated with it, they have at the same time recast their critique of Western civilization as a critique of Christianity, which supposedly lies at the very root of this civilization of exploitation. The mandate given to mankind to subdue the earth—that is, "theologization" of man's domination of the earth, his exploitation of the earth—has, according to this view, sent us down a fateful path, the bitter end of which is now becoming apparent. It was in the context of such ideas that Carl Amery coined the phrase: "the merciless consequences of Christianity".

What we once saw as cause for celebration—the de-mythologization of the world that came with belief in cre-ation, which made it subject to reason; the realization that the sun, the moon, and the stars are not powerful deities, but mere lights in the sky; the lifting of the shroud of mys-ticism surrounding plants and animals—all of these things are now seen as an indictment of Christianity. Christianity is said to have transformed the great powers of the world, once our brothers and sisters, into utilitarian objects for the use of man, leading to the misuse of plants and animals and the powers of this world in general in service to an ideology of growth and progress that thinks only of itself and cares only for itself.

The question is, is this true? What are we to say about this? Now, I do think our reflections so far have already cleared some things up, to where we really just need to elaborate a bit more. The Creator's mandate to man calls for him to in-habit the world as God's creation, living in accordance with the rhythm and the logic of creation. The meaning of the directive is paraphrased in the following, second, chapter of Genesis with the words "till it and keep it" (cf. Gen 2:15). It thus aims to engage with the language of creation itself; it means that it is to be made into what it is capable of being and what it is called to be, but not turned against itself. The faith of the Bible implies, more than anything else, that man is not closed in upon himself, that he must always be aware that he is situated within the great body of history, which will ultimately become the Body of Christ.

Past, present, and future should meet and permeate one another in the life of each person. Our own age is the first to experience the kind of narcissism that cuts itself off from both the past and the future and is preoccupied exclusively with its own present. And in any event, it is true that in this century, particularly since the thirties, theology, in its need to prove itself up to date and to justify itself, has tended toward interpreting the phrase "Fill the earth and subdue it" in a way that would justify such reproaches, but which nevertheless reflects a recent interpretation and not the original one.

But if this is the case, then that is all the more reason to ask how the excesses of this mentality of activity and domination that threatens us all today ever came about. I would like to highlight just a few things here. I think that the path that led to this point begins with the massive changes brought about by the Renaissance. That is to say, it starts with the return to pre-Christian Greek ideals, but by now the world has changed, and those Greek ideals are no longer embedded within a mythical framework. Instead, the demythologization of the world by Christianity is something that people take for granted; at the same time, however, they are also beginning to leave the Christian God behind, or to push him to the periphery, seeing him as a deistic God.

So this new path begins with the return of Greek ideals in a world that is no longer Greek; and, at the same time, with the rejection of the Christian worldview for the sake of the Greek. An example that is in some way quite symptomatic of this way of looking at things can be found in a statement by Galileo, who once said, essentially, that if nature does not voluntarily yield its secrets when we seek to wrest them from it, then we will subject it to torture and scrupulous interrogation; and in this wracking inquisition, for which we have the proper instruments, force it to give us the answers that we demand of it. That is quite an evocative definition of what would become of the natural sciences, with their tendency, as it were, to view nature as a criminal defendant who must be subjected to rigorous interrogation, even torture, if that is what it takes to produce a confession. However, it was not until after the Enlightenment that this new mentality acquired its concrete, epoch-defining form and then found its full political momentum with Karl Marx. Marx was the one who said that mankind should no longer inquire into its origins, to think about where we came from. According to him, this was a pointless question; it was all behind us anyway, so what good would it do us? Questions like that were not going to help us change the world. Marx would thus have us push aside the reasonable question about the "whence" of the universe that we spoke of at the beginning, because the reason inherent in creation offers the strongest and most unmistakable message from the Creator, from whom we can never fully claim our independence.

If the question of creation is such that there is no other way to answer it except by recourse to the Creator Intelligence, then the question is declared to be nonsensical from the very start. Creation, as such, does not matter anyway. After all, the point of philosophy is not just to contemplate things, but to inspire people to act. And it is precisely this basic turn that gives rise to everything else: to the idea that contemplation no longer has any value, that being free, that leisure no longer have any value because worship no longer has any value and that, therefore, action, changing the world, becomes the sole purpose of philosophy, which for its part is simply a guide to action.

And so, creation, as something accomplished, is of no

consequence. It is up to mankind to bring about the true creation, which will then be good for something. Hence, the fundamental task of mankind is change; and the real truth is progress; and for man, matter is not merely matter, but the material out of which human beings are to create a world that is worth living in.

It was Ernst Bloch and his talent for persuasion in his peculiar, poetic style who further elevated these ideas and presented them with more clarity. According to Bloch, truth is not what we take it to be. I think it is also important to note that in the context of a mentality that views not contemplation but action as decisive, not worship but change, not creation as such but the making of our own creation—within such a framework, the concept of truth would naturally have to be fundamentally different as well. The truth is not what we take it to be; rather, truth is what we do. Truth is change; truth is what ultimately gets things done. And reality, as he puts it, is a signal to invade and an instruction to attack.

It requires, as he again says, a "concrete hate-object" for us to find the necessary impetus for change. But then the beautiful, which is something that concerned him very much as a poetic type, is also something different from what we thought it was. For man, beauty is not *splendor veritatis*, as Thomas says, the inner radiance of the truth, the truth shining through things, but the glimmer of the future. What is beautiful is that which shows us a glimpse of what is to come, the future toward which we are moving and which we are ourselves trying to build.

And this is why he says that the "cathedral of the future will be the laboratory", that the "Basilicas of San Marco in the new era will be electric plants." Personally, I am glad I will never have to experience those times; because then, so he claims, people will no longer need to distinguish between Sundays and work days; there will no longer be any need for a Sabbath, because in every respect man will be his own creator. And he will also cease to be merely concerned with mastering nature or shaping it to his liking, but will understand nature itself as transformation. Here, perhaps precisely due to Bloch's skillful use of hyperbole or the directness of his poetic language, we find the very thing that threatens our age formulated with the rarest clarity.

Previously, man was only ever capable of changing certain things in nature. Nature as such was not an object of his activity, but a precondition for it. Now nature itself has been delivered into his hands in its entirety—or at least man thinks so. But as a result, he also suddenly finds himself exposed to the greatest danger he has ever faced. The origin of this danger lies in the attitude that views creation only as a product of chance and necessity, where the action of God no longer exists and all that remains is our own action. Since it appears to be nothing more than a product of chance and necessity, it is governed by no law, and no direction can issue forth from it; there is, at best, a mathematical, maybe even an aesthetic language to it, but there is no longer any moral language. And especially in recent discussions on ethics, we read again and again how the only direction we can derive from nature is that nature itself experiments and it selects.

That inner rhythm that we infer from the scriptural account—the rhythm of worship, the rhythm of the history of God's love for mankind—has fallen silent. Today, however, we are becoming increasingly aware of the horrible consequences of this way of viewing things. We sense a threat that does not lie in the distant future but is an imminent danger to us here and now. And I think this might actually also be the great opportunity of our time, as the arrogance of man as do-er is coming up against its limits, and it is once again becoming clear how much we need the humility that lies in listening and in beholding.

At the same time, there is a misguided kind of reaction of which we must be no less wary; namely, the reaction in the opposite direction, which is really just a feigned humility. This would be the attitude that sees mankind as a disruptive agent that wrecks everything and says that human beings are the true pest, the true disease of nature. The loss of the humility of being leads to the emergence of a perverse kind of humility, one in which man no longer likes himself, where he would rather just take himself out of the equation entirely. There is an increasing number of books being published with titles that call for the withdrawal of human beings from nature, the abolition of mankind. Man, so it goes, needs to take himself out of the way so that nature can be healthy again. But even by negating the created reality of man, we are not thereby restoring the world, since we are also going against the Creator when we no longer want to exist as the human beings whose existence he willed. And in turn, rather than healing the world, we end up destroying both ourselves and creation. We deprive it of the hope that lies within it and the greatness to which it is called, for it awaits the revealing of the children of God, as Romans 8 tells us.

And so in the face of so many opposing currents, the Christian path, if it is correctly followed, remains the way of salvation. Part of the Christian path is the conviction that the only way for us to be truly creative—that is, capable of creating—is by doing so in harmony with the Creator, with the One who made the universe. We can really only serve the earth if we receive it in accordance with God's Word, but in doing so we will truly be able to advance and perfect both ourselves and the world. "Operi dei nihil præponatur" —I come back to this statement once more and would like to conclude by saying that this sentence represents the true, dynamic "law of conservation" of creation, against the false worship of progress, against the false worship of change that tramples on human beings, and against the denigration of the human species, which likewise destroys the world and creation and keeps it from its ultimate goal. The Creator alone is the true savior of humanity, and it is only by trusting the Creator that we find ourselves on the path to saving the world, mankind, and all things.

# Man, the Divine Project

Let us now consider the question of man, which, for the Christian, leads to the question of Christ. What do we mean by "creation of man"? Now I do not intend to answer these questions on my own terms, of course but, rather, by thinking along with the words of Scripture. So please allow me to start by reading to you the passages that deal most directly with all of this.

First, we have Genesis 1:26–28:

> Then God said, "Let us make man in our image, after our likeness; and let them have dominion over the fish of the sea, and over the birds of the air, and over the cattle, and over all the earth, and over every creeping thing that creeps upon the earth." So God created man in his own image, in the image of God he created him; male and female he created them. And God blessed them, and God said to them, "Be fruitful and multiply, and fill the earth and subdue it; and have dominion over the fish of the sea and over the birds of the air and over every living thing that moves upon the earth."

In addition to this first, Priestly account of the creation of man, there is a second account in chapter 2, verses 4–7, which belongs to a more ancient source. Here is what it says:

> In the day that the LORD God made the earth and the heavens, when no plant of the field was yet in the earth and

no herb of the field had yet sprung up—for the LORD God had not caused it to rain upon the earth, and there was no man to till the ground; but a mist went up from the earth and watered the whole face of the ground—then the LORD God formed man of dust from the ground, and breathed into his nostrils the breath of life; and man became a living soul.

And so the question we are dealing with is: "What is man?", the question that imposes itself on every generation and on every individual person. For while the life of the animal is laid out for it in advance—it does not need to think about what it is going to do as a cow or as a cat or as a dog; it has a nature, and it fulfills its nature—the life of a human being is open-ended, and it can be decided one way or another. No one just knows what to do automatically; no one is simply presented with a ready-made path to follow; each person encounters it as a question, to which each person responds in a certain way, where even refusing to answer is itself still an answer. Being human is a task that is given to each and every one of us, an appeal to our freedom. Sartre portrayed this quite dramatically as the lot to which man is condemned: that, having no intrinsic nature, it is up to him to invent himself. While we should certainly object to the radicality of this view, even on empirical grounds alone, it remains true that what it means to be human is not something that is just predetermined for us. Rather, it is a question that needs to be explored anew, and each of us must decide who or what we wish to be as human beings.

Thus, the question "What is man?" is not a matter of philosophical theorizing but is the most practical question of all, the one that precedes all other questions and in all other questions is asked and answered.

Now this is where the biblical account of creation is situated, here at the very heart of the question "What is man?" That is, what it is concerned with are not other aspects of the question like how he functions in terms of biology and so forth, but this fundamental question: "What am I? What must I do to be a human being?" It seeks to guide us on our journey into the mysterious land of human existence; it seeks to help us discern what God's project with man is all about. Now by saying this, of course, I have already revealed part of the answer: Man is not merely some entity devoid of an essential nature; rather, God has a project planned for him, and he has freely entrusted man with the task of fulfilling this project, and doing so with creativity. And with this text, it is like God is rushing to our aid, trying to help us to give our own, creative response to the question that each one of us has to answer for himself.

So now that I have attempted to shed some light on the aim of this text, as it were, the next question for us to ask is: "What is it telling us?"

## Formed from God's Earth

So, as the account begins, we are told that God formed man from the dust of the earth. Now this verse, which we would probably put differently today, as we would understand this "dust" itself as a living, organic, reality—which nevertheless does not actually change anything—this verse is at once humbling and consoling. Humbling, because what it is telling us is: You are not God, you did not make yourself, and you do not have power over the universe; you are limited. You are a being destined for death, like all living

68      MAN, THE DIVINE PROJECT

things. You are but dust. But that which is so humbling at
first, reminding us of our limits, is also a consolation in that
it also tells us that man is not a demon; he is not an evil
spirit, though it might seem that way at times, and so many
mythologies say as much. Man is not formed from negative
forces, from dragon's blood and dragon's flesh, but has been
fashioned from God's good earth. And behind this glimmers
something deeper yet, for we are told that this applies to all of
mankind—that is, all human beings are earth. By no means
has this always been evident to everyone, and it eludes many
even today. It is cultural criticism at its most serious, since
it means that despite all of the differences brought about by
culture and history, the fact remains that we are all, in the
final analysis, the same. The medieval notion expressed in
the "dance of death", which arose amid the terrifying experience of death as universal menace during the great plague
epidemics of the period, was already present in substantial
form here in this account. Emperor and beggar, master and
servant—in the most profound sense they are all one, one
and the same man, taken from one and the same earth and
destined to return to that same earth. Throughout all the
devastation and great achievements of history, man remains
the same. He remains dust, from which he is formed and
to which he is destined to return.

    Thus, in the very first instance of the Bible's discourse
on man, what it immediately emphasizes is the unity of the
entire human race. We are all from only *one* earth. There are
not different kinds of "blood and soil". There are not fundamentally different kinds of human beings, as imagined by the
myths of so many religions and that various ideologies assert
even in our day. There are not castes and races of different
value into which human beings can be divided. We are all
one humanity, formed from God's one earth. And this basic

idca, thc first basic motif of Scripture, where it begins the story, so to speak, lies at the heart of the Bible and remains a continuous theme throughout it: in the face of all the divisions and all the arrogant pretensions of man, whereby one sets himself over and against the other, mankind is declared to be one creation of God, formed from his one earth. What it says at the beginning here is then repeated after the Flood, in the great genealogy of Genesis 10, which returns to the notion that all men are but one, that among the many different people there is only one "man", making the rejection of racism in all its forms, of any attempt to divide up mankind, into one of the earliest and most fundamental truths of the Bible.

## The Breath of God

So now, we have considered how the image of "earth" is used to illustrate how man is formed from the soil. But for man to become *man*, a second thing needs to happen. The base material is earth, but man comes into existence only after God breathes his breath into the nostrils of the body formed from the earth. That is to say, this is where divine reality enters the world. The first creation account, which I read to you previously, says the same thing expressed here by the image of God breathing his breath into man. It does so by way of another, more deeply reflective image, in its claim that man is created in God's image and likeness. The meaning here is the same—in man, heaven and earth come into contact with one another; in man, God enters into his creation; man is in a direct relationship with God. He is called by him. God's words in the Old Testament apply to each and every human being: "I have called you by name, you are mine" [Is 43:1]. Every person is known and loved by God, each one is willed by God, and each one is made in God's image.

And it is here that this idea of the unity of mankind, which I just expressed in terms of the element earth, first takes on its full dimensions and the true breadth and depth of the claim become apparent: for beyond our common origin and our common destiny, the earth, it is now saying that each of us, every single human being, is the fulfillment of *one* Divine Project. That the origin of every human being lies in the same creative thought of God, which of course (since each is in direct contact with God) is personally revealed in each of them. And it is because every human being is in a direct relationship with God, because each one is a direct idea of God, that Genesis 9:5–6 says that whoever commits an offense against man is committing an offense against God. Human life stands under God's special protection, as it is there that his breath is present. Every person, however wretched or exalted he may be, however sick and suffering, however useless or however important, whether born or unborn, whether terminally ill or brimming with life—each one bears God's breath within him; each one is God's image.

This insight, that man is not some accidental product of the earth, but that each is a divine project, that he is in a direct relationship with God, is, in the final analysis, the sole supporting reason for the inviolability of human dignity, and thus it is upon this fact that every civilization ultimately rests. Wherever this idea is abandoned, wherever man is no longer understood to be under the protection of God, no longer seen as having God's breath inside of him, then over time it becomes quite natural to begin classifying him according to his utility, according to whatever standards lend themselves to the society in question.

And so it is where this happens, where man is no longer viewed in terms of this personal adjacency to God and, thus, under the immediate, inviolable protection of God, that the kind of barbarism that tramples on human dignity appears. For this is the very dividing line between civilization and barbarism—whether there is unconditional respect for man or not. Conversely, this means that where this respect is present, though many things may happen that are wrong, there is a clear recognition of the fundamental value of man, moving such a society beyond the threshold of barbarism and toward something positive.

## Human Dignity and Ethics

The fate of us all, then, especially in this age of cultural transition, depends on whether this moral dignity of man is something we can defend, something we can reexamine and renew our commitment to living out in the world of technology, which *per se* thinks in terms of what is usable, what can be quantified, what serves a practical purpose. For there is a particular temptation that is distinctive to our age of science and technology; the technical and scientific attitude has produced a particular kind of certitude—namely the kind that can be confirmed by experimentation and mathematical formulas. Here is a way of proving things that does not permit any dissent, since anyone can demonstrate it for himself. It has thus given mankind a certain freedom from anxiety and superstition, a certain power over the world. And that is a positive thing. But now there is a temptation to view only that which can be corroborated by experiment and calculation as reasonable and therefore worth taking seriously and, where this kind of exclusivity arises, to regard only this kind of certainty as reasonable at all. But this turns something good, the benefit of knowledge, into an attack on man. For it means that the moral and the sacred, which after all cannot factor into this kind of thinking, no longer count. They are relegated to the domain of things that need to be overcome, things that are irrational. But wherever people do this, it means reducing the ethical to the physical; this is what is going on in a whole series of ethical models today, such as proportionalism, for instance: good and evil become a question of calculating the potential consequences. Where the ethical is reduced to the physical like this, where man no longer accepts any limit on what he *may* do, but sees the limit on what he *can* do as the only limit at all—and anything that *can* be done *may* be done—then we extinguish the essence of what makes him truly human. For it is precisely in his recognition of moral limits that man enters into contact with God. And by taking away these limits, which in reality are what open him up to eternal things, we extinguish the true essence of man; consequently, we do not liberate him, though it may seem that way at first. If moral limits are taken away, man will push the boundaries of what he is able to do farther and farther out. What we are actually taking from him is the dimension that is the breath of God. And in doing so, we do not liberate him, but, rather, under the appearance of liberation, we destroy the very thing in him that makes him infinitely valuable and inviolable.

This is why I believe that the truly crucial challenge of our hour in history is to recognize again something that was still recognized by Kant at the beginning of the turn in the Enlightenment, which he reformulated in new and grand terms: namely, that there are two fundamental "promises" of reason, the theoretical and the practical, as he puts it.

Based on what we have been talking about, let us go ahead and say physical, scientific reason and moral-religious reason, each of which has its own way of seeing things. We cannot declare moral reason to be irrational and superstitious, a mere first step toward something that needs to be scientifically verified and incorporated into the realm of science and its forms of certainty as soon as possible, simply because it is of a different nature and the insights it offers are something other than mathematical in character.

On the contrary, Kant insists, and rightly so, that it is the greater form of reason, which, precisely because it is oriented toward something greater, cannot grasp it in the same way. It is that form of reason which alone can safeguard the proper status of science and technology in human affairs and prevent them from becoming mankind's destruction. In purely technological terms, it is progress if I am able to produce weapons that are increasingly effective in their destructive power. It is only when the human standard of what man ought to do, and to what end, is added that the dignity of what is other can be preserved as well.

Kant, then, still spoke of the primacy of practical over theoretical reason and said that the deeper, most significant realities are those that are recognized by the moral reason of man, who possesses moral freedom. For this, we now add, is the domain of man's being made in the image of God; it is what makes man more than "earth", that alone entitles him to exercise dominion over the earth, since he then does so according to the standard of God, which means maintaining and not destroying. And if I take away this standard, then indeed he no longer has any right to any form of dominion, either.

## Image of God

Now let us take this a step farther. We are currently in the process of interpreting this second element, "breath of God —image of God", and I am now going to attempt to explore the concept of "image" a bit more. What is an image in the first place? What is it that makes something an image? I think the essence of an image lies in the fact that it represents something, or at least that it expresses something in some form. When I see it, I recognize, say, the person or the landscape it depicts, or I am at least asked to go beyond the materials themselves, to inquire more deeply, to explore it. In other words, the image points to something else outside of itself. The essence of an image lies not in what it *is* in itself (oil, canvas, frame, etc.); its essential nature as an image lies in the fact that it points beyond itself, that it shows something, touches on something that it, in itself, is not.

With this in mind, we can now try to understand what it means when Scripture says that man is the image of God. Being made in the image of God means that man cannot be closed in on himself. That there is more to him than just what he, in himself, is. If he tries to remain closed within himself, he will never be able to find himself. If he desires only himself, he will lose himself. Therefore, being made in the image of God means, in a word, relationality. This is the dynamic that moves man beyond himself and toward that which is other than himself, toward those who are other than himself, and ultimately toward him who is entirely Other. In this sense, then, being made in the image of God means having the capacity for relationship. Now, if man's true dignity, that which defines him as man, lies in his being made in the image of God, this means that man is most profoundly human when he steps outside of himself, when he becomes capable of addressing God with the familiar "Thou".

And so in response to the question "What actually distinguishes man from animal—what is it about man that is so new and special?", we must therefore say: He is that being which God has given the ability to think, the one that can go beyond all the things of this world and reach out to the Other. We might say that he is the one being that can pray; that is, not only can he think of God, but he is also capable of entering into a relationship with him.

In this case, man is most profoundly himself when he steps outside of himself, when he discovers his relationship to his Creator. Because of this, being made in the image of God also means that man is a being of the Word and of love, a being of movement toward the other, meant to give himself to the other and, only in the act of real self-giving, truly to receive himself back.

## The Second Adam

We can go one step even farther in interpreting this idea if we go ahead and apply our basic rule—that is, if we remember that the Old and the New Testament need to be read together and that it is only in the New Testament that the deepest sense of the Old is revealed.

The New Testament calls Christ the second Adam, thus consciously referring back to the texts we have just read. And because he is called the second Adam, or the last Adam, he is then also emphatically called "the image of God", *eikon tou theou*. This means that it is in him alone that the full answer to the question "What is man?" is to be found. It is only in him that the innermost content of this project is revealed. He is the ultimate man, and all of creation is, as it were, a preliminary sketch that points to him. Consequently, we can say that man is that being that can become a brother of Jesus Christ. He is the creature that can become one with Christ and, in him, with God himself; he is able to receive not only relationship, but unity.

Hence this relation of creature to Christ, of the first Adam to the second, indicates that man is a being on a journey, a being characterized by transition. He is not yet entirely himself, but he first needs to become so in a definitive sense.

And so, if we are looking at the Bible as a whole, then here in the midst of our thoughts about creation we are suddenly confronted with the Paschal Mystery, the mystery of the grain of wheat that has died. Like the grain of wheat, man must die with Christ in order truly to rise, truly to stand upright, truly to be himself. Only then does he become what he was actually designed to be.

In other words—and once again I think this is very important in light of what we have been thinking about—man is not to be understood only in terms of his past or in terms of the isolated moment that we call the present; he is oriented toward his future, and it is only from the perspective of his future that who he is is fully revealed. Hence, we must always see the human person as someone with whom we will one day share in God's joy. We must see him as someone who is called, together with us, to become a member of the Body of Christ, alongside whom we will one day sit at the table of Abraham, Isaac, and Jacob, the table of Jesus Christ, thus becoming his brother and, with him, a brother of Jesus Christ, a child of God. I believe that if we always keep in mind the ethical and spiritual instruction entailed here in the Christological idea that we are made in the image of God, it will have a tremendous effect on the smallest details of our everyday lives. Always to see man in terms of his future, as the one with whom we will one day sit at that table, knowing that we will never reach the destination until we become capable of doing so.

## Creation and Evolution

So now we have explored the theological elements of "earth" and "breath" and attempted to explain what these two concepts are telling us. All well and good, we might say, but is not all of this ultimately refuted by our scientific knowledge of man's descent from the animals? Well, to begin with, I would say that more thoughtful minds have long recognized that this is not a matter of either-or. If we are correctly understanding both concepts, then we cannot really say "creation *or* evolution". What we should actually be saying is "creation *and* evolution", as these two things are responses to two different questions. The story of the dust of the earth and the breath of God does not in fact tell us how a human being comes to be; rather, it tells us what a human being is. It tells of man's deepest origin and sheds light on the project that undergirds his existence. Conversely, the theory of evolution attempts to recognize and describe the biological processes at play, but it cannot explain where the "project" of man comes from, his inner origin, or his particular nature. To that extent, what we are faced with here are two complementary—rather than mutually exclusive— questions.

So that is a general explanation to start with. Still, I do

think we need to look at this issue a bit more closely, because here, too, the progress of thought in the past two decades can help us to grasp anew the inner unity of creation and evolution, of faith and reason.

First, let us go back to the origin of these theories in the nineteenth century, as the theory did develop in a particular context, after all. One of the particular insights of the nineteenth century was an increasing understanding of the historicity of all things, the idea that all things had *become* what they were. We began to realize that things that we had always taken to be unchanging and immutable in kind were the products of a long process of becoming, and we could, as it were, accurately describe the nineteenth-century scientific process as one in which all things were historicized, expanded into their historical dimensions; and this insight, whereby things that previously appeared unchanging now appear to be the products of a process of becoming, applied to the human realm as much as it did to nature. It became evident that the universe was not something like a big box, into which everything was placed in a finished state, but was rather more comparable to a living, still-growing tree, gradually lifting its branches higher and higher into the sky.

This general idea was nevertheless often interpreted in rather fantastic ways, and to some extent still is, but with the advance of scientific research, it has become more and more apparent how it is to be legitimately understood.

Of course, the scope of the debate over this very issue has become quite convoluted and wide-ranging, making it necessary to pick and choose which parts of it we are going to focus on, though we should nevertheless attempt to take certain characteristic elements into account.

## Chance and Necessity

Let me begin by briefly saying something in connection with Jacques Monod, whose reputation as a highly regarded scientist and scholar, on the one hand, and as resolute opponent of any belief in creation, on the other, certainly lends credence to his testimony. As I said before, even if many of the details have become outdated in the course of scientific advancement, by no means does that invalidate the basic elements that make up his argument.

Monod underscored two fundamentally important clarifications, and I think it is important for us to begin there. The first one says that there is more to reality than that which is necessary. Remember, the title of his most famous book is *Chance and Necessity*. Reality, as we see it, is made up of both of these elements, and, contrary to the attempts of Laplace and Hegel to imagine otherwise, it is not possible to derive all things in the universe in a chain of ineluctable necessity. That kind of necessity does not exist. There is no "world-formula" that would necessarily lead to everything that is; rather, there are both necessity and chance in the universe. As Christians, we would take this a step farther and say there are necessity and freedom, but then we would be adding another philosophical dimension, and we do not need to go any farther down that road right now. Suffice it to say that there are those things that must be from the start, so to speak, and there are those things that do not necessarily have to be.

Monod indicates that in the universe that is accessible to us, there are two realities in particular that we must say had the potential to be—that is, the conditions for existence were such that they were a possibility—but did not necessarily have to be. The first of these two realities—remember, these are those that always could have been, but did not necessarily have to be—is life. Given the laws of physics, it was possible for life to emerge, but it did not actually have to. He even adds that it was highly unlikely for this to happen. The mathematical probability for it was close to zero, such that one might even assume that this highly improbable event, the emergence of life, may well have only happened this one time on our earth. Even if we were to assess the degree of probability differently, what matters is that something that was able to come about based on the composition of matter, but which did not have to, is not necessary.

The second thing that had the potential to be but did not necessarily have to be is the mysterious being known as man. Man, too, is improbable given what we started with—so improbable that Monod the scientist determines that the degree of probability is such that it was practically impossible for this being to have emerged more than once. "We are an accident", he says. We drew a lucky number in the lottery and should view ourselves in the same way that we would view someone who has suddenly and unexpectedly won billions in a game of chance. He is thus expressing in his own words what the faith of the ages has called the contingency of man and what, for the faith, has become a prayer: "I did not have to be, but I am, and you, O God, have willed me."

It is just that in place of God's will, Monod posits that we are the result of chance, of the lottery. If that were so, then there are very good reasons to doubt whether we can actually claim that the lot we have drawn is a winner.

Once when I was taking a taxi from Fiumicino airport to Rome, I struck up a conversation with the driver, who told me how he had noticed more and more young people telling him, "No one ever asked me if I wanted to be born!" This is obviously meant as a reproach and is in no way an expression of gratitude or joy over winning the lottery. And —I know I have told this story more than once as well— one time after a confirmation a teacher told me that he had tried to get a difficult child who was always fighting with his parents to be more grateful to them by saying, "Still, you do have them to thank for the very fact that you exist in the first place, and there is nothing more important than that." To which the boy responded, "But I'm not thankful for that at all, since I do not even want to live." To him, being human was not winning the lottery. And indeed, if we have been cast into an ocean of nothingness by nothing but the blind chance of a lottery, then that is reason enough to conclude that we have drawn the short straw.

It is only when we know that there is One who did not cast lots blindly, when we know that our existence is not an accident, but is rather born of freedom and love, only then can we, whose existence is not necessary, be thankful for this freedom and know, with gratitude, that it is indeed a gift to be human.

But now let us take a closer look at the question of evolution and the mechanisms involved in it. Microbiology and biochemistry have given us revolutionary insights on this front, yet they have also opened up ever larger and more impenetrable questions. They are constantly penetrating more deeply into the innermost mysteries of life, seeking to decode its secret language and to understand what this thing called life actually is. In the process, they have come to recognize that, in very many respects, an organism is comparable to a machine, as the two things have much in common. After all, they are both the realization of a project, a functioning and therefore well-planned design that is coherent and logical in itself. We function in that we are able to see, to speak, to hear, and so on; a machine functions by printing or producing something. The functioning of both depends on a sophisticated and therefore thought-provoking design —this is what they have in common. They are both deliberately intended projects with a certain intended function. But in addition to this commonality, which allows us to say that the organism is a kind of machine, Monod catalogues a series of three differences. The first of these, rather trivial in comparison to the others, is that "project organism" is incomparably more clever and audacious than even the most sophisticated machines. Machines are clumsily designed and constructed in comparison with the project that is an organism. A second difference goes deeper: "Project organism" is self-operating, acting from within, not like a machine, which needs to be operated by someone outside of itself. And finally, there is the third difference: Project organism has the power to reproduce itself. It is able to renew and pass on the project that it itself is. In other words, it has the ability to propagate itself, bringing into existence another living, coherent whole like itself.

Now this, however, brings up something quite unanticipated and very important, what Monod calls "the platonic side of the universe". That is to say—and this is one of the fundamental, perhaps *the* fundamental observation of modern biochemistry: there is not only becoming, in which all things are constantly changing, but there is also permanency; what he means are those perpetual projects, those perpetual ideas that shine through reality and serve as its constant guiding principles. There is such a thing as permanency, and it is so constituted that every organism reproduces its pattern, the project that it is. And it is really quite exciting to read such a resolute atheist and, in some respects, anti-philosopher like

Monod saying that the more we learn, the more it seems that the most dedicated Platonists have it right that nature is rigorously structured in accordance with stably enduring ideas. An organism, he says, is conservatively designed and, in propagating itself, reproduces itself exactly. And thus, as he puts it, evolution, as understood by modern biology, is not a specific property of living beings; rather, their specific property is that they are invariant. They pass themselves on; their project endures. Of course, then the question is, if the intrinsic quality of living things, so to speak, is that they are representatives of a set project, which they pass on as such—then where exactly does the variance, the evolution, the progress in the organic world come from?

This is a matter of some controversy. I need not go into the details here, nor by any means could I. So I will stay with Monod, who finds the possibility for evolution in the observation—which is undisputed—that the act of propagating the project, which is in itself the conservative reproduction of the same, unchanging idea, may result in transcription errors. But because nature is conservative, these errors, once they exist, continue to be passed on. Errors of this nature tend to add up, and the accumulation of such errors can result in the emergence of something new. Up to this point, this is all just a matter of empirical fact, but now comes the bewildering conclusion: It was by this means—by the accumulation of transcription errors—that the entire world of living things came about, including man. We are the product of a random accumulation of errors.

This too, I believe, is an incredibly profound diagnosis and itself an image of the human person. How then are we to respond to this?

Well, first of all, I think we ought to accept the limits of our competence here. That is, it remains the business of the natural sciences to explain the particular factors by which the tree of life grows and expands, the specific details surrounding any other potential factors apart from errors that supplement, as it were, the conservatism and the "Platonism" of nature. To inquire into these individual factors is not a matter for faith. But given all the knowledge we have, we can and should have the courage to say that the great projects of living existence are not the product of external happenstance, whatever the factors involved. Nor are they the product of a selection process to which one may attach divine attributes, which in this place are illogical and unscientific, a modern myth. Reading such texts, it is clear that the very use of nature as a subject—it *does* this and that—is an attempt to obscure something that this use of the subject is unable to hide—that we are dealing with a myth. The great projects of living existence, whatever specific factors helped to bring them about, point to One who has projects, point to a creative Reason. They show us the Creator Intelligence, and they do so more luminously and radiantly today than ever before.

## The Divine Project

Thus we can say with newfound certainty that, yes, man is indeed a divine project and not an accumulation of transcription errors. Only the Creator Intelligence was powerful enough and great and audacious enough to conceive of such a project. Man is not a mistake, but is willed; he is the fruit of love. He can look within himself, into the audacious project that he is, and discover the language of the Creator Intelligence, who speaks to him and gives him the courage to respond: Yes, Father, you willed me to be.

Allow me to conclude these reflections by coming back to

Christ as the ultimate manifestation of the human project, from the point of view of the Passion, considering how, as we gaze on the Pierced One, we are gazing at God's project with regard to man. After the Roman soldiers had scourged Jesus, crowned him with thorns, and clothed him in a cloak of mockery, they led him back to Pilate. And this hardened politician and skeptic was apparently still capable of being moved on a human level by this image, clearly shaken by the broken and shattered human being before him. Hoping to arouse pity, he presents him to the crowd with the words: *idou ho anthropos*—"Behold the man!" But as the Evangelist meant it, it should probably be: "See here, this is man, this is what man is!" Thus, as Pilate uses them, these are the words of a cynic trying to say: We take such pride in being human, but look, here he is; this worm, *that* is man, how contemptible, how small he is.

But John the Evangelist nevertheless saw something prophetic in this cynic's words and handed them down as such to the Christian faith. Pilate is right to say, "Look, this is man." In Jesus Christ we can discern what man, this project of God, is and how it is that we engage with this divine project. In the ill treatment of Jesus, we can see how cruel, how small, how low man can be. In him we can discern the whole history of human hate, of the wretchedness of human sin. But even more, it is in him and in his suffering love for us that we are able to discern clearly God's response. Yes, this is man, beloved by God even down into the dust, so beloved by God that he pursues him even to the final privation of death. Even in his greatest humiliation, he is still the one who is called by God, and God stands by him; brother of Jesus Christ and chosen to share in God's eternal love.

The answer to the question "What is man?" is not found

in a theory but in following Jesus Christ, in living this project with him who is the answer. By following in his footsteps day by day, patiently living and suffering with him—and only in this way—we can learn what it means to be human and, thus, become human ourselves.

# Sin and Redemption

Going through the topics in the order in which I planned
them, we should now be coming to "Sin and Redemption".
And since I want to ensure a solid textual basis for this topic
as well, please allow me to read from the first half of the
third chapter of Genesis so you will have it in mind as a
reference point for the ideas we will be discussing:

> Now the serpent was more subtle than any other wild crea-
> ture that the LORD God had made. He said to the woman,
> "Did God say, 'You shall not eat of any tree of the gar-
> den'?" And the woman said to the serpent, "We may eat
> of the fruit of the trees of the garden; but God said, 'You
> shall not eat of the fruit of the tree which is in the midst of
> the garden, neither shall you touch it, lest you die.'" But
> the serpent said to the woman, "You will not die. For God
> knows that when you eat of it your eyes will be opened,
> and you will be like God, knowing good and evil." So
> when the woman saw that the tree was good for food, and
> that it was a delight to the eyes, and that the tree was to
> be desired to make one wise, she took of its fruit and ate;
> and she also gave some to her husband, and he ate. Then
> the eyes of both of them were opened, and they knew that
> they were naked; and they sewed fig leaves together and
> made themselves aprons.
>
> And they heard the sound of the LORD God walking in
> the garden in the cool of the day, and the man and his wife
> hid themselves from the presence of the LORD God among
> the trees of the garden. But the LORD God called to the

man, and said to him, "Where are you?" And he said, "I heard the sound of you in the garden, and I was afraid, because I was naked; and I hid myself." He said, "Who told you that you were naked? Have you eaten of the tree of which I commanded you not to eat?" The man said, "The woman whom you gave to be with me, she gave me fruit of the tree, and I ate." Then the LORD God said to the woman, "What is this that you have done?" The woman said, "The serpent beguiled me, and I ate." (Gen 3:1–13)

Now before we go on, let me point out that the same interpretive framework that we established for Genesis 1 applies here as well; that is, we need to keep in mind the unity of Scripture and, more than anything else, read it with Christ. Thus, this text should always be read together with Romans 5, where Paul talks about how sin entered the world, and it is from there that it receives its Christian interpretation.

So that was just to give you some idea of the textual basis for the things to which I will be referring, though of course our reflections today are only going to cover a small part of it, and that in rather broad strokes.

## "Repent!"

As I was planning this lecture and thinking about what I wanted to discuss, I recalled a little scene from the first meeting of the Council of the Bishops' Synod after the Synod on the Family. We were attempting to take stock of things and evaluate what had taken place at the synod and determine how things had gone, and at the same time we were supposed to be exploring topics for the next synod from among those that had already been suggested before coming

up with a concrete proposal. In the course of these efforts—
that is, trying to recognize what issues in the Church today
are of such a nature that they need to be handled by a synod,
or which questions should be given priority over the many
others that there are—we ultimately ended up turning to
Scripture for direction. As we tried to identify some words
that might guide us, we soon came across the classic passage
in Mark 1:14–15, in which the Evangelist sums up the entire
theme of Jesus' message and, thus, the fundamental theme
of every form of evangelization. This is the verse that says:
"The time is fulfilled, and the kingdom of God is at hand:
repent and believe in the Gospel."

For a moment, our discussion became a sort of Bible study
on this text, and one of the bishops from another continent
said something that really moved me, something that has
stayed with me since then, etched into my memory. What
he said was that he felt as though for a long time we had
been taking the message of Jesus, summed up as it is in this
passage, and actually cutting it in half. We love to talk a
lot about evangelization, about the Good News, in order to
make Christianity attractive to people, and that is a good
thing. But in the process we are leaving a part of it out,
he said. Too many people these days lack the courage to
profess the prophetic message "Repent!" in all its serious-
ness; that is, the part that comes before the words "believe
in the Gospel." Almost no one, he said, is truly willing to
proclaim this elementary call of the Gospel to our age, this
call by which the Lord wants to make us recognize that each
one of us is a sinner, that each one of us is guilty, that we
need to repent and to acknowledge that we need to become
someone else, that we must begin to change the world starting with ourselves. Then, with that characteristic vigor that
comes more naturally to non-European people than to us, so

wrapped up as we are in the abstract, the bishop added that all too often, the way we preach the Christian message today sounds like a recording of a symphony where the opening bars and the first major theme have been cut out, leaving the whole symphony amputated, its inner progression unintelligible. What then grew out of these discussions was indeed the theme of the next bishops' synod, "Penance and Reconciliation".

## Strategies of Suppression

With this discussion, we were touching upon a major sore point in our present-day situation within the history of ideas. The matter of sin, even more so than creation, I think, has become one of those things that are no longer spoken about in our age. We do our best to avoid it in our preaching and teaching. It is used ironically in theater and film, or played for entertainment, and as Josef Pieper has said, a word that has become a hit in operettas and films has, as it were, fallen out of normal usage. Sociology and psychology attempt to unmask it as an illusion or a complex; even in matters of law, there have been increasing attempts to make do without the notion of guilt, and you are beginning to see greater use of ideas from sociology, which, rather than seeing the concepts of good and evil as two different fundamental qualities of human behavior, views them purely in terms of statistics, distinguishing between normative and deviant behavior, whereby deviant behavior is simply that which a society punishes in order to preserve the norm. But if that is true, then the difference between good and evil is ultimately just a statistical one, which also means, of course, that the statistical proportions can be reversed, and what is deviant today could one day become the rule. Indeed, we may even have a good reason for wanting to see them reversed; that is, to see the deviant actually become the norm, perhaps because it is more useful. By reducing things to the quantitative in this way, which, in ethics, corresponds to the theory of proportionalism—that is, the reduction of good and evil to the weighing of consequences—we are thus essentially abandoning the whole concept of moral right and wrong.

In this view, moral right and wrong is regarded as an idea that does not really serve any purpose but to torment people and is to be dismissed altogether and replaced with practical codes of conduct for a given society. And indeed, if there is no standard that precedes man, if there is no standard that is intrinsic to him, if he is not in keeping with any concept, any project, but just invents himself as he goes along, if he does not exist until we create him; that is to say, if we cannot say that there is an inner language to creation itself, then it makes perfect sense to dismiss morality altogether as a genuine dimension of human existence.

But now we have arrived at the actual heart of the matter. For precisely to the extent that reason is one-dimensional, where only one dimension of reason is considered scientifically valid, the idea of an intrinsic human standard no longer makes any sense and ultimately becomes an idea that man sees as a kind of affront, as an arbitrary threat to his freedom. He knows of no standard to which he is held and does not want to know of one, either, precisely because such a standard would limit the possibilities available to him. This situation reminds me of the words of Simone Weil, a French Jew, who really hit the mark when she said, "We experience good only by doing it. . . . When we do evil we do not know it, because evil flies from the light."[1] Or, in a nutshell: we only recognize good when we do it and only recognize evil when we do not do it. In a similar vein, Goethe once said that one only recognizes a mistake as a mistake after one is rid of it.

Given the prevailing intellectual climate in which we currently find ourselves, it makes a certain amount of sense that the topic of sin is one that has been suppressed, yet it nevertheless remains quite real. The symptoms of this are manifold—one that I have noticed has become increasingly prevalent in our society is this aggressiveness where people are always ready to pounce, this ever-ready willingness to insult the others, to blame them for our own misfortune, or to condemn society as a whole and seek to change the world through violence. It seems to me that the only way to understand all this is to understand it as an expression of the suppressed reality of guilt, which man does not want to acknowledge. But since it is nevertheless still there, he has to attack it and crush it. And because man suppresses the truth but is unable to do away with it, he becomes sickened by this suppressed truth. This is why Jesus says that it is the task of the Holy Spirit to "convince the world of sin" (Jn 16:8). When we hear this, it bothers us at first. Why, we might ask, do we need constantly to accuse people of sin? But the point of this is not to make people's lives miserable or to box them in with restrictions and negative prohibitions; the simple fact is that it is meant to lead them to the truth and, thus, to heal them. For man can only be whole if he is true, if he stops suppressing and crushing the truth.

---

[1] Simone Weil, *Gravity and Grace*, trans. Gustave Thibon (1952; Lincoln: Univ. of Nebraska Press, 1977), p. 121.

The third chapter of the book of Genesis, the text on which we are basing our present reflections, is, it seems to me, one instance of this action of the Holy Spirit that permeates all of history. He convinces the world, and us, of the reality of sin, not to humiliate us, but to make us true and therefore healthy, in order to save us. Once again, the text speaks in images; what it says is something that can likewise only be represented in images, as it transcends our ability to grasp it fully. This chapter is dominated by two images in particular: one is the image of the garden—and this includes the image of the tree—and the other is the image of the serpent.

## Two Images: The Garden and the Serpent

The garden is the image of a world that is not a wilderness, a danger, or a threat to man, but his home, which shelters, nourishes, and sustains him. That is, the garden is an expression of a world that bears the imprint of the Spirit, of a world that came into being in accord with the will of the Creator. Thus, there are two currents running through it that interact with one another: the first is the one whereby man does not exploit the world, does not selfishly dominate it, does not seek to make it his own private property apart from God's creative will, but recognizes it as the gift of the Creator, building it up to what it was created to be and bringing out its true potential. The other current, which operates in response to this one, is that whereby the world, created in a state of unity with its Lord, is not a threat to man, but a gift, a sign of the saving and unifying goodness of God.

The image of the serpent is taken from Oriental fertility

cults. Thus, it stands in the first place for those fertility religions that had for centuries been Israel's main temptation,
the great and real danger of abandoning the covenant—to
go back to before the covenant, so to speak, and to immerse
itself in the general religious climate of the era. For that was
indeed Israel's greatest and all-too-understandable temptation—to shed its unique status among the nations and to
become like the others. Speaking through the fertility cults,
the serpent says to man: Stop clinging to this distant God
who has nothing to offer you. Stop clinging to this covenant
that is so alien to you and imposes so many limits on you;
immerse yourself in the flow of life, in the intoxication and
ecstasies it offers, and you yourself can share in the reality of
life and in its immortality, in its divinity, and become wise.

At the time in which the Paradise account was given its
final literary form, there was a tremendous danger that Israel, seduced by the proximity, the sensuality, and the spirit
of these religions, would adopt them and that the distant-
seeming God of promises and creation would thus disappear
and be forgotten. Set against this historical background, the
text is a lot easier to understand; for example, in the account of the prophet Elijah, we learn that Elijah was the
only prophet of Yahweh left in the land, as compared to
thousands of prophets of Baal. To them, the religion of
Yahweh was essentially too complicated, too distant, too
troublesome, a holdover that would soon be entirely ab-
sorbed into the great flow of religion from the Orient and
all that it promised. Eve saw how delicious it would be to eat
from this tree, saw what a feast for the eyes it was, tempting
her to become wise. In this respect, the story also illustrates
a very concrete historical constellation of ideas. In those
religions, the serpent symbolized wisdom, which rules the
world; knowledge, which is power; and fertility, in which

man is immersed in the divine flow of life, momentarily aware of his oneness with its divine power. Thus the serpent becomes the symbol for the allure that these religions represent to Israel as compared to the mysterious nature of God's covenant.

## The Logic of Suspicion

And so it is against the backdrop of the temptation of Israel that Sacred Scripture depicts the temptation of Adam and, thus more broadly, the nature of temptation and sin in every age. Temptation does not begin with the denial of God, with the fall into outright atheism. The serpent does not deny God; rather, he begins with a simple question, one that appears quite sensible on the surface. In reality, though, there is a certain insinuation contained within the question, and as it draws man into this insinuation, it undermines his trust, instills suspicion in him, and diverts his fundamental orientation from one of trust to one of mistrust. All the serpent asks is: "Did God say, 'You shall not eat of any tree of the garden'?" It is a rather harmless question, and in itself it appears to be perfectly legitimate. And yet, in the way it is asked, it puts a new face on reality, raising doubt about the prohibition, about the limitation that has been placed on man.

So it begins, not with the total loss of faith, not with anything like a direct affront against God, but with something quite harmless, a slightly one-sided piece of information, a suspicion of the covenant, of the community of faith and the ordinances of that community, a suspicion of the commands that enable man to live in accordance with the God of the covenant. And, indeed, suspicions of this kind

—not of God himself, but suspicions toward the covenantal order, the covenantal community—are always understandable. If one begins to suspect that these things represent a restriction on freedom, and if obedience to the covenant is suddenly perceived as a fetter that prevents us from enjoying the things that life really promises, then such doubts are very likely to arise. It is easy to convince man that this covenant actually keeps him shackled and is not an infinite gift, but an expression of envy toward man that robs him of his freedom and the most precious things in life.

Once he becomes suspicious of the covenant, man is on his way toward building his own world. In other words, implicit in this suspicion is the proposition that man should not view the limits imposed by good and evil, by morality, as limitations at all, but should rather liberate himself from them, for only then will he be truly free of these things. This suspicion of the covenant and the accompanying invitation for man to free himself from his limitations has appeared in various forms throughout history and is the defining feature of the present-day intellectual landscape. While this basic temptation has presented itself in many guises throughout history, I am only going to discuss two variations that are particularly prevalent today: the aesthetic and the technological.

## May Man Do Whatever He Can?

Let us start with the aesthetic variation, which likewise begins with a very simple question: "What may art do?" The answer appears to be quite simple—art may do whatever is artistically possible. It needs only one rule, and that is itself, artistic ability. And the only error that can be made with respect to it is artistic error, the lack of artistic ability, which makes it non-art. From this it follows that there are, say, no good books or bad books, there are only well-written books and poorly written books; there are only well-made films and poorly made films. What is good, what is morally right does not matter; these are alien categories that have no place here. The only thing that counts is skill, artistic achievement, for art is based on ability. Anything else is a violation—perfectly plausible, given the premises.

But on a deeper level, if we are going to be consistent, what this means is that there is at any rate one area where man is able to rise above the limitations placed on him. When he makes art, there are no limitations on him, and he can do whatever it is that he is capable of doing. And this means that the sole measure of man is what he can do, not what he is, not what is good or evil. Whatever he *can* do, he *may* do.

The significance of this is much more evident today— and its effects much more radical and urgent—with respect to the second variation, the technological one. Still, it is a variation on the concept and refers to the same reality, as, after all, the Greek word *techne* means "art" in English, and the same idea of "being able" is implied here. So here, too, we might ask: "What may technology do?" For a very long time, the answer seemed perfectly obvious: It may do what it can do. The only error that it recognizes is that of incompetence. Robert Oppenheimer relates that when the atomic bomb first emerged as a possibility, nuclear physicists such as himself were mesmerized by the lure of "the technically sweet"—the desire to do, and the thought of actually doing what was entering the zone of the achievable, the technologically possible, was like a magnet to which they could not help but be drawn.

Rudolf Höss, the last commandant of Auschwitz, wrote in his diary that the extermination camp was an unprecedented technological achievement. They had to take into account the ministry's timetable, the capacity of the crematoria, their burning power, etc., and to bring all of this together in such a way that it functioned so smoothly amounted to a fascinating and well-coordinated program that justified itself as such precisely because of its technological fine-tuning. One could continue at length with similar examples, but the production of all the horrors that continue to multiply as we look on with incomprehension, and, in many cases, helplessness, nevertheless have this one thing in common, and that is the question: Is there any other limitation on man apart from what he is able to do? Our whole intellectual situation, our restriction of reason to technical-scientific reason, necessarily leads to the gradual disappearance of any other limit, to the gradual disappearance of what *may* be done as an acceptable limit, making it seem as though the only limitation on man is what *can* be done.

But in reality, this is to deny that there is any limit whatsoever, since of course the limit to what we *can* do is never more than a practical, momentary one, and all human endeavors are supposed to be directed toward expanding this limit ever farther, giving us the ability to do more and more, and ultimately to do away with this limit altogether, to the point where we are able do everything, becoming omnipotent like God. But then this denial of the reality of good and evil as a standard, a limitation, placed on man means that power becomes the only reality that matters anymore, and all of human behavior is reduced to doing. In other words, it denies being as a reality that precedes us and defines us in order to focus on freedom alone, which, for its part, is understood as the freedom of power, the freedom to do.

Being, createdness, and creation arc cclipscd by act, by that which is done.

This reminds me of an idea developed by Erich Fromm, whose account of "being and having" included the notion that our culture is a culture of having, but that which is had is, by its nature, dead, meaning that our civilization is one of death and of dead things. And the more time passes, I think, the more deeply and thoroughly evident this becomes. What is done is, by its very nature, dead, and thus it just goes to show once again that a civilization that dismisses being in favor of doing and of power is a civilization of death. We can see how very true the statement "Do this, and you will die" turns out to be—not in the sense of instantly falling over dead, but in the sense of giving oneself over to the dominion and the power of death.

And so, looking at the consequences of this principle— that man ought to recognize what he *can* do as the sole limitation on himself and should no longer accept what he *may* do as a limitation—in looking at the consequences of this principle, we should begin to recognize once more that this is a deception from the serpent and that it is destructive to both man and the world. We should understand that man can never retreat into a place where skill and ability are all that count. And so at all times, the measure of man is man himself, is creation, is good and evil, and when he rejects this standard, he is deceiving himself. He is not freeing himself, however much it appears to be so in the moment; rather, he is placing himself in opposition to the truth. He is lying, and that means that he is destroying both himself and the world and, thus, entering the realm of death, of untruth, of non-being.

## Creatureliness as the Measure of Man

This, then, I think, is the first and most fundamental thing that the story of Adam tells us about the nature of human guilt and, therefore, our entire existence: the order of the covenant is placed into doubt. This is how it always begins, and not with a direct affront against God. The God of the covenant, so near to us, is cast aside and, with him, the limitations imposed by good and evil, the limits of what we *may* do, and the inbuilt measure of human existence, of man's "creatureliness". We could almost say, in fact, that the very essence of sin is man seeking to deny his creatureliness, as he does not wish to accept the truth that there is a standard or limitations placed on him. He does not want to be a creature, as he does not want to be subject to a standard, does not want to be dependent.

This of course sheds light on another factor of this strategy of suspicion, which is that man perceives his dependence on God's creative love as an imposition on himself from without. But an imposition from without is slavery, and slavery is something from which man must free himself. Thus, man is no longer able to see this love for what it really is, but is only capable of viewing it as dependence, as an imposition on his own will, and from this he can only wish to seek his emancipation and to become God himself. And it comes as no surprise that, wherever he tries to do this, it changes everything. Man's relationship to himself is altered, as is his relationship to others and his relationship to the world. To someone who wishes to be God, who wishes to be dependent on no one, who wants to have no limitations and not be subject to any standard, to such a person, the other is naturally perceived as a hindrance, as a rival, as a threat. Likewise, his relationship with the other becomes one of mutual recrimination and struggle, as the Paradise account so masterfully illustrates in the dialogue between God and Adam and Eve, where each one now regards the other as the guilty one. Adam says, "the woman gave it to me," and the woman says "the snake gave it to me." Because they deny the standard in this way, their relationship with one another becomes one of accusation, of struggle, of competition.

Man's relationship with the world is altered as well, becoming one of destruction and exploitation, for the man who regards his dependence on supreme love as slavery and seeks to deny the truth about himself—that he does not exist of himself, but through love; that he is a created being— does not become free but, instead, destroys truth and love. Rather than making himself God, which he cannot do, he makes himself into a caricature, a pseudo-God, a slave of his own abilities, which ultimately become his downfall. So it is now clear that sin is, in its very essence, a renunciation of the truth. The person who will accept no limits on himself, who does not want to be what he is, is denying the truth. And thus now we can understand another aspect of what I attempted to explain earlier, which is what is meant by those mysterious words "when you eat of it"—that is, when you deny the limits placed on you, when you deny that you are subject to a standard, then "you shall die" (Gen 2:17). This means that those who deny the limitations imposed on them by good and evil, the standard built into creation, are denying the truth and are living in untruth, in unreality. To them, life becomes an illusion, a web of untruths, subject to the dominion of death. This, too, I think, is something on which we have a fresh perspective today, living as we do in a civilization that has become, to a certain degree, a civilization of death and of killing. In a world of untruth, a world of unlife, we know the extent to which death holds sway, negating even life itself and turning it into a kind of death.

### What Is Meant by "Original Sin"?

Now, the Genesis account that we are currently discussing adds a further characteristic to our description of the nature of sin. To begin with, we can say that the specific temptation represented by the serpent reflects a kind of phenomenology of sin, through which the nature of temptation and sin in general is made manifest. But that is only the start. Another thing is that it describes sin, not in general as an abstract possibility, but as an actual deed, as the sin of Adam, who stands at the beginning of mankind and with whom the history of sin begins, though the character of this deed is not fully expressed until Romans 5—that is, its New Testament *relecture*. This is because it was not until the moment when our salvation was made known to us that it even became possible to come face-to-face with the full reality of the danger that sin represents, the horror of it all. It is not until the point at which we are given the answer that the rest of the picture is fully revealed. And so, read in this way, what the account tells us is that sin begets sin, and, therefore, all the sins of history are linked together.

To describe this state of affairs, theology has come up with the certainly misleading and imprecise term "original sin". So the question is, what do we actually mean by this? After all, nothing seems to be more alien, indeed, more absurd, to our modern sensibilities than to claim that there is such a thing as original sin. According to our understanding, guilt can only ever be something incredibly personal. God does not run a concentration camp, punishing family members for the crimes of their relatives, but is the liberating God of love, who calls each of us by name. So the question is, what does original sin mean, if we are interpreting the term correctly? To answer this would require nothing less than acquiring an accurate understanding of man, and of course all of our efforts to that end are bound to be insufficient. I think that before anything else, it needs to be stressed that no man is closed in on himself, that no one is capable of living entirely of himself or for himself alone. We receive our lives each day from without, from others who are not ourselves yet relate to us in some way. Man's self is not contained only within himself but exists almost even more so outside of himself. He lives in those on whom he loves, in those on whom his life depends, and in those for whom he lives. Man is relational, and his life, his very self, only exists by way of relationship. I, by myself, am not "I" at all, but am so only in relation to a "Thou", and it is the "Thou" that makes me myself.

To be truly human means to subsist in the relationship that is love, love *of* and love *for*. But sin means—and it is only now that we can properly describe it—sin means to disrupt or to destroy this relationship. This was essentially our key insight before, if you remember. Sin is the denial of this relationship, because it seeks to make man into God while assuming an erroneous image of God, as if God were the One without relationship, whereby one would be God if one were fully self-contained and autonomous. And so inasmuch as sin is the intent to become God, and to do so according to a false image, sin is precisely the attempt to become self-sufficient, to sever every form of dependency, every instance of relationship. By its very nature, because it is the loss of the truth, sin is the loss of relationship, the disruption of relationship, and therefore sin is never confined

to the individual self alone. Sin is the disruption of relationship, and if I disrupt the relationship, then this will necessarily affect others in that relationship—that is, the whole.
The consequence of this is that sin is always an offense that
affects others, that alters the world and disrupts it.

And because this is so, then it follows that if the relational fabric of human existence is disrupted from the very
beginning, then every human being will henceforth enter
into a world characterized by relational disruption. At the
moment we receive our human existence, which is good,
we also inherit a world disrupted by sin. Each of us enters into an interconnected web where the relationships are
distorted, starting with our relationship with God. Consequently, each person's relationships are disrupted from the
very beginning, and he does not receive them as they are
meant to be. Sin takes hold of him, and he goes along with it.

## Redemption and the Relationality of Creation

So now it should also be clear that man is incapable of re-
deeming himself, as the frustration and failure of his existence—the alienation he experiences, we would say today
—come down to the fact that he desires himself alone, and
the more he reduplicates this, the more radical his alienation
becomes; that is, the more and more he is removed from
his nature. We can only be redeemed—that is, we can only
be free and true—if we stop wanting to be a god, when we
renounce our delusions of autonomy and self-sufficiency.
We can only ever *be* redeemed. Only when we accept our
passive role may we enter into the realm of salvation, of
freedom, and of truth. Or, to rephrase that: We become
ourselves, each one becomes himself, when we receive the
proper relationships and accept them. But to have proper

relationships with other human beings, we must first have a balanced sense of our own creatureliness; yet it is precisely here that the disturbance lies, since our relationship with creation has itself been disrupted. For this reason, only the Creator himself can be our redeemer. We can only be redeemed if he from whom we have cut ourselves off approaches us again and takes it upon himself to reopen the relationship, something that we cannot force. For the very idea that we could force it is of course once again a denial of the relationship that is love. Only to be loved is to be redeemed, and only the love of God can purify disrupted human love and restore the vast web of relationships that has been alienated from its very foundation.

Thus, the Old Testament account of the beginning of mankind reaches beyond itself, raising questions and expressing hope as it points toward the One in whom God endured our refusal to accept our limitations and subjected himself to our standard in order to bring us back to ourselves. The New Testament response to the Fall of man—that is, another New Testament text that we need to read alongside Genesis 3 in order to understand it properly—is most succinctly and emphatically summed up in the pre-Pauline Christ hymn that Paul incorporates into his Letter to the Philippians. The Church has rightly placed this text at the center of the Triduum liturgy, that is, the celebration of the Paschal Mysteries, the events surrounding our redemption. Allow me to read you the key passage here:

"Have this mind among yourselves, which was in Christ Jesus, who, though he was in the form of God"—and those who know what the word *morphe* means in Greek will know that this actually means he was equal to God—

> though he was in the form of God, did not count equality with God a thing to be grasped, but emptied himself, taking

the form of a servant, being born in the likeness of men. And being found in human form he humbled himself and became obedient unto death, even death on a cross. Therefore God has highly exalted him and bestowed on him the name which is above every name, that at the name of Jesus every knee should bow, in heaven and on earth and under the earth, and every tongue confess that Jesus Christ is Lord, to the glory of God the Father. (Phil 2:5–11)

We do not have time to consider this text in detail, but I thought I should point out how, here too, the Old and the New Testament provide the key to interpreting one another and how it is only in light of their intertwined nature that either can be properly understood. And while I do not intend to explain everything here, I would like to focus on a few points of relationship between them, limiting myself to the connection between this text and the story of the Fall, to which it clearly alludes when it says "Jesus did not count equality with God a thing to be grasped."

Nevertheless, we should probably also assume that he was thinking of a somewhat different tradition of the Fall, such as the one that appears in Job 15:8, which presents the first man as having tried to steal God's divinity from him. So the hymn alludes to a slightly different version of the story of the Fall, the story of Adam, than the one we have in Genesis 3. But in terms of substance, it is dealing with the same thing.

Now what the hymn tells us is that Jesus walked the same path as Adam—who wished to elevate himself and become God, who wished to appropriate divinity for himself by casting off his fetters—but in reverse. Unlike Adam, he truly is like God, but precisely because he is truly like God, he behaves himself like the true God and not like someone who wants to be God and ends up degenerating into a caricature.

For to truly "be like God" is to be a Son, and hence it is totally relational. The Son is nothing on his own, which is how the Gospel of John describes this "Son-ness". He is totally and completely relational, and precisely because he is entirely relational, he is equal to God. Therefore, because it is the case that true equality with God and precisely not closed-off self-sufficiency and self-possessing and self-making is the radical form of love, this of course means that the One who is truly like God does not cling to his autonomy, to the limitlessness of his abilities, of what he is able to do, what he is willing and able to put into action, but goes the opposite route. He becomes the One who is completely dependent, because it is not the path of power that he walks, but that of love. And because of this, he is able to descend into the depths of Adam's lie, into the depths of death, and, there, raise up truth and give life. Thus, in this countermovement, which at the same time recapitulates the whole story and gathers it together again, Christ becomes the new Adam, with whom mankind begins anew and finds itself once more, he, who is by nature relationship and relationality, such that his very name is a relational word. A son is someone who is defined by his being from someone else. He who is himself relationship and relationality restores relationships and reestablishes relationship as such.

The Gospel of John also contains that other wonderful image, where his outstretched arms are his open invitation to the relationship that he offers to us always. "And I, when I am lifted up . . . , will draw all men to myself" (Jn 12:32), for then I am all relationship, no longer with the Father alone, but with you. And it is when we allow ourselves to be taken into this relationship that what is lacking is transformed, history is transformed, God acts. In this way, the Cross, the place of his obedience, becomes the true tree of life, and life is the regaining of the relationship that is life. Christ thus becomes the antitype of the serpent, as John explicitly indicates elsewhere in his Gospel, chapter 3, verse 14, where Jesus references the story of the bronze serpent in the desert, which of course for its part was already a cultic transformation of the story of the serpent in Paradise. What Jesus says is that in that story, people were healed by looking at the serpent, but the serpent is *I*, and I will heal from the tree on which I will hang. From this tree will come not words of temptation, but the word of love that saves; the word of obedience, in which God himself has become obedience, obedience in his very being, thus offering his obedience as the space of freedom. Thus, in the symbolic language of John's Gospel, which draws the whole complex of the Paradise account into its Christology, the Cross is the tree of life, which can now be approached once more. In his Passion, Christ has, as it were, removed the fiery sword, passed through the fire, and has raised the Cross as the true central axis of the world.

## Eucharist as "Tree of Life"

This means that the Eucharist, as the presence of the Cross, is the abiding tree of life that we may approach, standing ever in our midst and inviting us to receive the fruit of true life. But at the same time, this also demonstrates the tremendous magnitude and drama of what the Eucharist is. It shows that the Eucharist can never be merely a way to foster community, but that to receive it actually means to enter into this dynamic transformation of the story of Adam, to eat from the tree of life. And this means to receive the crucified Lord, to accept the parameters of his life, his obedience, his obedience to being, to creation, and to the Creator, the standard of our creatureliness. Not to rely on power and on doing, on what we *can* do, as the sole limitation on ourselves, to be overcome some day, but on the relationship that is love and on the standard that it offers us. In other words, to celebrate the Eucharist means to go to this tree, to cast our gaze upon the new serpent, to accept the love of God, which is our truth, to accept that dependence on God that is no more an imposition from without than is the Son's sonship.

It is this very dependence that constitutes our freedom, because it is truth and love. The chance to look upon the Pierced One, which is offered to us as the response to the devastating conversation with the serpent; to gaze upon the new serpent, on the Living One, should free us from the spell of the serpent's gaze, from our desire to be able to *do*, from our desire to be God on our own, and help us to free ourselves from our denials, from our suspicion of the covenant and the covenant community, from our rejection of standards and the lie of our self-determination, and point us toward the Tree of Life, which is our standard and our hope. I believe that inasmuch as this is accomplished, the words of Jesus with which we started will once again be made present in their entirety: "The kingdom of God is at hand; repent, and believe in the gospel" (Mk 1:15).

# The Ecclesiology of Vatican II

I would like to start by elaborating a few general principles centered around the basic idea "Ecclesiology of Vatican II". This discussion is bound to be very incomplete, of course, as this is a topic that could easily take several weeks to cover. Then in my next lecture, I would like to develop some thoughts on the topic of "Plurality and Unity in the Church".

Now if we are going to talk about the ecclesiology of the Second Vatican Council, we cannot just begin in 1962. It is not like the council and its pronouncements were created at a single moment in time, after all; rather, they are the fruit of a process of growth and maturation, one that, in its entirety, naturally extends back through the whole history of the Church. However, it is really after the First World War that we get to its more proximate historical background, so in order to get a reasonable understanding of what we are dealing with, we should go ahead and trace each of these lines of thought from that point on. The hiatus in theological thought brought about by the First World War was described back in 1921 by Romano Guardini, whose words would become quite well-known and frequently cited, as he indeed described the overall feel of the period between the two World Wars as it pertained to the Church. His famous line was: "A religious process of incalculable importance has begun—the Church is coming to life in the souls of men."[1]

---

[1] Romano Guardini, *The Church and the Catholic*, trans. Ada Lane (New York: Sheed & Ward, 1935), p. 11.

We might say that Vatican II was the fruit of this awakening; it put into words and shared with the whole Church the insights, born of faith, that had matured in the four decades full of awakening and hope between 1920 and 1960. Therefore, as I have already indicated, I would like to proceed by attempting to outline the ideas that were being developed during those years in order to show how each one then feeds into the council and takes shape there, forming the central points of the Church's conciliar teaching.

## Church as "Body of Christ"

Consequently, if we are going to proceed in this genetic and non-systematic way, one of the first key terms that we will need to deal with is that phrase which dominated the era between 1920 and 1940—namely, "body of Christ". "The Church is coming to life in the souls of men"—Guardini had chosen his words quite deliberately here, since what mattered to him was precisely that the Church was now being recognized as something alive *within* ourselves, something internal to us; it does not come to us from without like some external apparatus, but lives within our very selves. If the image of the Church that had been dominant until that time was largely a juridical one—that is, "Church" was seen primarily in structural and organizational terms; as an institution, people used to say—now a new view had emerged: We ourselves are the Church. She is more than an organization; she is something that is alive within us, she is the organism of the Holy Spirit, who embraces us all in his living presence. This new perception of "Church", that the Church is not to be found in institutional apparatus and juridical structures, but is present where faith is lived, that it is alive within us because it is the organism of the Spirit—this new awareness found apt expression in the phrase "Mystical Body of Christ". At the time, this expressed a departure from an essentially legalistic and institutional understanding of the Church in favor of a new and liberating experience, of which Guardini once again wrote movingly near the end of his life, in the same year that Vatican II's Constitution on the Church [*Lumen gentium*] was promulgated. In 1965, he published a book called *Die Kirche des Herrn: Meditationen über Wesen und Auftrag der Kirche* (The Church of the Lord: On the Nature and Mission of the Church). Guardini begins this book with a recollection titled "Between Two Books", in which he traces the arc between the start of this movement and its culmination, drawing on the wisdom and maturity of a life dedicated to the Church to describe once more the fruit of his thought in view of Vatican II, which was then already underway. In this little book, he once again articulates the experience of that era, through which he was presently living, and which he felt was important to pass on to the future: that as long as we view the Church as an organization that serves specific ends, as an authority that stands in opposition to individual freedom, as an assemblage of people who share the same views and attitudes on religious matters, we still do not have the proper relationship to her; rather, the Church is a living reality, and our relationship to her must itself be life.

Today it is difficult to communicate the enthusiasm and the joy that accompanied such an insight at the time because we are unable to relate to the intellectual climate of the era. The era that preceded World War I was the true age of liberalism, an intolerant liberalism at that, and one that viewed the Catholic Church in particular as a relic of unenlightened times that needed to be overcome. This led to an inferiority complex among Catholics themselves, who felt compelled to set themselves apart, at times militantly, from the prevailing zeitgeist and the dominant forces of the age. This in turn resulted in a certain narrowing of thought in many areas, but it also led to great bursts of vitality. When it came to theology, the marginalization of Catholics in the age of liberalism went hand in hand with the need to work out the legacy of Vatican I, so that theological thought regarding the Church automatically centered on the analysis of the papacy and papal primacy; and here, too, the focus of such thought very much revolved around the organizational and juridical aspects of the Church and her central institutions. The end of the First World War was an epochal turning point in that it marked the collapse of the age of liberalism, offering a whole new sense of relief to many Christians, who suddenly found themselves being called upon by history once more. In the course of this new awakening, it became apparent that the Church is much more than a central institution, that in our faith, we all carry on her life together, just as she carries us. It became clear that she has grown and developed organically through the centuries and that this growth continues even today.

If you think about, say, Gertrud von Le Fort's *Hymns to the Church*, this is another expression of this new experience, this new joy at this power that cannot be crushed by any world war, at this living thing that is capable of enduring catastrophes of all kinds. All of this enabled people to see and, indeed, to experience once more how the mystery of the Incarnation remains ever-present in the Church. That it gets its constancy, its reliability in the face of all upheavals from the very fact that Christ still has a body in the world and that he continues to walk on through the world in all its miseries across the ages themselves.

Now, to conclude this brief attempt at a history lesson, let us ask ourselves: What elements from that first new awakening persisted and found their way into Vatican II? We could say that the first of these things that endured and emerged as one of the basic themes of Vatican II is the Christological definition of the concept of Church, the notion that Christ is the "first word" of the Church. On that note, we will have to go back another hundred years or so. You see, there had also been a reawakening of Catholicism at the end of the Enlightenment and the Napoleonic era, much like the one after the end of the First World War, and this awakening also garnered a great deal of interest. The great promoter of all this in the nineteenth century was Johann Adam Möhler, whose writings also mainly focused on the Church, at a time when people were digging up all these lost concepts. Möhler once said that a kind of false theology could be summed up in the phrase: "In the beginning, Christ established the hierarchy, and thus did more than enough for the Church until the end of time." According to Möhler, this is a caricature, and we should counter this idea—that this was something he did in the past and that was enough—with the truth that the Church is the Mystical Body of Christ. What this means is that Christ did not just establish the Church once and for all and hand her over to the hierarchy, but that he himself is founding her ever anew, that he is never merely in the Church's past, but, most significantly, he belongs to her present and her future as well. In the Church, Christ is always in the present—he is contemporaneous with us, and we exist simultaneously with him. This was another thought that accompanied Guardini throughout his life as he struggled with Kierkegaard, whose main question, as you may recall, was: "How can I, a man of the nineteenth century, live contemporaneously with Christ, for only then am I a

Christian?" Kierkegaard never did actually come up with a proper answer. For Guardini, the answer was that *this* is where he lives alongside us, that it is in the Church that we are contemporary with him. She lives from the presence of Christ in our hearts, and it is from there that Christ forms his Church for himself, and not the other way around. And it is precisely because of this that the first word of the Church is Christ and not herself. She remains healthy to the extent that all her attention is focused on him.

Vatican II magnificently placed this insight at the forefront of everything it had to say about the Church by beginning its Constitution on the Church with the words *Lumen gentium cum sit Christus*—"Christ is the Light of nations." Because Christ is the Light of the World, there is also the mirror of his glory, the Church, which reflects his splendor and communicates it to the world. If we want to understand Vatican II properly, then this is the phrase to which we need to keep coming back; and I often note that many people think this phrase *Lumen gentium*, "Light of the nations", is referring to the Church. No, the opening words of this text rightly refer to Christ, and it is only from this standpoint that we can properly understand the Church. So to sum up: The first element from this new awakening we have been describing that has lived on is the Christological definition of the life of the Church.

The second thing arising from this beginning that we should take note of is the idea that the Church has both an aspect of interiority and an aspect of communality. The Church grows outward *from* within, and not the other way around. What "Church" means more than anything else is communion with Christ in the life of prayer. She takes form in the life of the sacraments, in the fundamental attitudes of faith, hope, and love. So when someone asks, "What must

I do for the Church to grow and to advance, for there to be progress in the Church?" the answer should be, "Do all that you can to ensure that there is faith, so that hope and love may flourish." Prayer is what builds up both the Church and the communion of the sacraments; in the sacraments, her prayer comes to meet us, so that the two streams of prayer flow into one another and therein become "Church".

This reminds me of a little experience I had this past summer. While on holiday in Upper Austria, I visited a parish near the border with Bavaria. The pastor related to me that when he took over the parish some fifteen or twenty years before, he was saddened to learn that the parish had not seen a single religious vocation as far back as anyone could remember, and he decided that the most important aspect of his ministry would be to see his parish become a source of vocations once more. But the question was, how was he supposed to do such a thing? It is not like we are able to manufacture vocations, after all. We can do everything in our power, but the only way the seeds are ever going to grow is if the Lord himself sows them. He thought about it and decided to make a yearly pilgrimage on foot over to Altötting to bring his intention to the Marian shrine for which the region is known, and to invite anyone who shared his intention to come along and pray with him. Year by year, the number of people who made the journey had grown, and I could still see the joy on his face as he described how this past year, their first new priest said his First Mass, and that there were more on the way. That is to say, he had been able to see firsthand how the Church grows. Certainly, what we do, how we act is important, but the essential reality is that she grows when we allow the Lord to give her to us and, indeed, when we approach him ourselves. So this is one example of what it means to say that the Church is the

"Body of Christ", but this phrase implies something else, too: Christ has formed a *body* for himself, and I must fit into it as a humble member, as there is no other way for me to find him or to have him. Yet in this way he is entirely mine, because by actually becoming one of his members, I have now become his organ in the world and, thus, for all eternity. The liberal idea, expressed by Adolf von Harnack and so many others, that Jesus is interesting but that the Church herself was a failed enterprise, utterly falls apart in the face of this insight. Christ exists only in his body and never purely as an ideal, because "incarnation" means precisely that I can have him only in his body and not in an idea. I can never have him apart from others, for myself alone; only together with the abiding communion that continues to walk through the ages, which is this body of his.

But then the next thing that necessarily follows from this is that the communal character of the Church, her guiding character, necessarily implies a "we". The Church is not located somewhere in space—we ourselves are the Church, and this was another of those great, joy-filled insights: that "we are the Church", but no one can say "I am the Church." Everyone can and should say, "we are the Church", and this "we" is not some group that isolates itself and says, okay, we twenty or however many of us there are, we are it and the others are all wrong—rather, it is a community that places itself within the whole communion of all the members of Christ's Body, the living and the dead. But when they do this, when they place themselves there, then they can truly say, "We who are here right now, *we* are the Church." "Church" is then present in this open "we" that breaks down barriers both social and political, but also the barriers between heaven and earth. "We are the Church" —this insight has given rise to a sense of shared responsibility and participation in the work of the Church, as well as the right to criticize, though at the same time, this always must always imply self-criticism as well, because once again, "Church" is not someone else, nor is she somewhere else; we ourselves are the Church. Likewise, these notions of the "we" character of the Church and the concrete nature of this "we" are also ideas that matured and developed right into the council. Everything that was said about the shared responsibility of the laity, all of the juridical structures that were created in order to facilitate the intelligent exercise of this responsibility, grew out of this, because now we say not only that it is up to the hierarchy to take care of things, but that it is up to *us*. And so we are all called to take responsibility for the Church, and the attempts to provide concrete juridical structures to allow this to function as a living reality are essentially all just ways of implementing this basic idea and this fundamental insight.

Finally, another idea that belongs to the legacy of this period leading up to the council is that of development and, thus, the dynamic nature of the Church throughout history. A body maintains its identity over time precisely because it is constantly renewing itself in the process of living. If this process of exchange, of renewal, stops happening, if it becomes rigid and frozen in place, that does not mean its identity becomes fixed; rather, it begins to disintegrate, as it has reached its end. This is the dynamic in which identity operates. Here it becomes necessary to turn back to the nineteenth century once more, for though it belongs to the more distant past than our period, it prepared the ground for those later awakenings. Thus it was with Cardinal Newman, for whom it was the idea of development that acted as the actual "bridge" toward his conversion to Catholicism. He realized that Anglicanism was essentially based on the idea that it could close the door on the history of the Church at a certain point in time, putting a stop to this dynamic of development; conversely, it was only the Catholic Church, which embraces all of history, that was capable of conforming to the inner essence of what was meant by "Church": identity that remains constant amid the constant dynamic of development. And I am of the opinion that the concept of development is indeed one of the most crucial basic concepts in Catholicism and that if we wish to define what is Catholic, then it is something on which we absolutely need to reflect. I also think that nowhere near enough has been done to make people aware of this concept and to help them to understand it with the depth and the clarity that the importance of the matter warrants.

But here, too, it is to the Second Vatican Council that we owe the credit for formulating this concept of development for what is, as far as I know, the first time in a solemn magisterial document—the one on Divine Revelation [*Dei Verbum*]—and also for emphasizing that this approach is central to Catholic identity. For it is indeed true that if someone tries to find his way based on the literal words of Scripture alone, telling himself that the rest does not concern him; or perhaps casts the net a bit wider, clinging to the standards laid down by the Church Fathers and nothing else, then what he is doing is banishing Christ to yesterday. The consequence of this is then either a romantic archaism, a completely sterile faith that has nothing to say to our times, or an arbitrary mindset that skips right over two thousand years of history, tosses it into the dustbin of misunderstandings, and says, "Well, none of them got it, but *we* understand Scripture now, and we have figured out what Christianity is actually supposed to look like according to Scripture—or to Jesus." But ultimately, all this can ever amount to is an artificial product of our own making that lacks any inherent stability. For there to be genuine identity with the origin, there needs to be a living continuity at the same time that unfolds this origin and, in doing so, preserves it.

## Eucharistic Ecclesiology

Now let us take this a step farther: We have seen how this first phase of the Church's internal rediscovery concentrated on the concept of the Mystical Body of Christ, which had been developed based on Saint Paul, and placed special emphasis on ideas about Christ's abiding presence and the dynamism of a living organism. But now we need to look at how, after this initial wave of enthusiasm, it became necessary to explore the question in greater detail. Having just drawn on Guardini and his contemporaries, we now need to consider a French theologian, Henri de Lubac, the man who could easily be considered the most influential Father of the council, who supplied it with three other fundamental concepts. First, he reexamined the word "Catholicism"; his first and perhaps most significant book is titled *Catholicisme*. Then, he was also the first to come up with the phrase "sacrament of the Church", which we are going to come back to later; and finally, he wrote a monograph of exceptionally wide-ranging scholarship on this very phrase, *corpus mysticum*, thereby calling attention to it. Paul, after all, does not write about the *corpus mysticum*, but simply the "Body of Christ"; he was not familiar with the term "mystical", as it does not appear until later and originally refers to the Eucharist, as the word *mystikon* means something like "sacramental" and not "mystical" in the modern sense. The crucial contribution that de Lubac now made was to point out that the phrase *corpus mysticum* originated as a title for the Most Holy Eucharist and to show how the Fathers were all in agreement with Paul on this. For both the Apostle and the Church Fathers, the idea of the Church as the Body of Christ would have been inseparable from the idea of the Eucharist, in which the Lord is present in his Body, which he gives us to eat. This insight, that the phrase "Body of Christ" always points to the Eucharist and that using it in reference to the Church can teach us to understand the Church in terms of the Eucharist, led to the emergence of a Eucharistic ecclesiology, which would later also come to be known as *communio* ecclesiology. This *communio* ecclesiology, I would say, actually became the core of what Vatican II had to say about the Church, this new thing given to us by the council that nevertheless draws radically from the earliest sources; it is from this core that all other aspects are evaluated and ordered.

What do we mean by Eucharistic ecclesiology? Again, I will try to outline very briefly just a few key points. The first is that Jesus' Last Supper now becomes recognizable as the true act of founding the Church. How does the Church come about? Jesus gives the liturgy of his death and his Resurrection to his disciples, thus bestowing on them the feast of life. At the Last Supper, the texts make it very clear, he is renewing the covenant of Sinai—and so here, too, the Old and the New Covenant are woven together. Or, to put it in more proper terms: What started out only in signs now becomes reality in the most unimaginable way; namely, the communion of blood and of life between God and mankind. Saying this, it is clear that the Last Supper anticipates the Cross and the Resurrection and that it necessarily presupposes them, as otherwise this would all remain an empty gesture. This is why the Church Fathers could say, using a very beautiful image, that the Church was born from the open side of the Lord, which poured out blood and water. In reality, this is the same thing, though from a different point of view, as when I say: "The Last Supper is the beginning of the Church; this is where the Church begins." For either way, what it means is that the Eucharist, the celebration of this sacrament of his death and his Resurrection in the signs of bread and wine, unites people who do this together, and it unites them in a communion not only with one another, but with the very One who is giving himself to them, with Christ, and that in this way it makes people into the Church. This also gives us the fundamental constitution of the Church; that is, the dualism between law and life, between law and love, between mysticism and institution—it is all resolved here. Now what we have just considered is in the deepest sense, as it were, the mystical content of the Church, of being a Christian, but, as such, its basic juridical form as well; for this means that "Church" is always born of "Eucharist", that it is in Eucharistic communion that the Church lives. Her liturgy, her worship service, is her constitution, for by her very nature she is the service of God and, therefore, also the service of man and service for transforming the world. The liturgy is both her form and her content at the same time. To say that it is her form means that there is within her an entirely unique relationship of multiplicity and unity that does not occur anywhere else. In every celebration of the Eucharist, the Lord is indeed present in his entirety; he is risen, and he is no longer subject to death and cannot be broken into pieces. It is not the case that everyone gets some piece of him; rather, he always gives himself whole and undivided. That is why the council says, and here I quote:

"This Church of Christ is truly present in all legitimate

local congregations of the faithful which, united with their pastors, are themselves called churches in the New Testament. For in their locality these are the new People called by God, in the Holy Spirit and in much fullness (cf. 1 Thess 1:5) . . ." "In these communities, though frequently small and poor, or living in the Diaspora, Christ is present, and in virtue of His presence there is brought together one, holy, catholic and apostolic Church." That quotation is from *Lumen gentium* 26.

If we try to put that in more concrete terms, what it means is that it is based on this Eucharistic approach to ecclesiology that Vatican II develops its characteristic ecclesiology of the local churches and explains the inner, sacramental basis for the Church's teaching on collegiality, which we will need to get to in a moment. Thus, the teaching on local churches was not something developed for tactical reasons, out of a need for decentralization or something like that; rather, it derives from this innermost reality, if "Church" is, so to speak, communion of Christians, Body of Christ. If it is through the Eucharist that she is this, if she is always grounded in the Eucharist, then this is the form she has, she is alive in each of the individual communities where the Eucharist is celebrated.

But really to get a proper understanding of what the council is teaching, we will need to take a closer look at the passage I just read. In this passage, we see how Vatican II was motivated by its own inner logic to deal with intellectual stimuli then coming from Orthodox and Protestant theology, which it nevertheless integrates into a larger, Catholic view. For it should be noted here that the concept of Eucharistic ecclesiology was first expressed in the work of exiled Russian Orthodox theologians in Paris after the First World War, who contrasted it with what they perceived to be the centralism of Rome, saying, more or less: "Rome's ecclesiology is based on the centralism of the papacy, the ecclesiology of Orthodoxy is Eucharistic in its form." Thinking in these oppositional terms, they then said that each Eucharistic congregation is wholly Church; there is nothing lacking, because, indeed, they have Christ in his entirety, and of course it is impossible to have any more of him than that. For this reason, so they concluded, outward unity with other communities that celebrate the Eucharist—that is, the horizontal unity of the local churches with one another—is not a constitutive element of the Church, and therefore it is not necessarily required. Each Eucharistic congregation has Christ fully, and—so this idea went—in that respect each one of them is fully the Church. Unity with the other congregations is not a constitutive element, and therefore—quite logically, given the premise—unity with Rome cannot be a constitutive element of the Church, either, and to demand this can only be indicative of arrogant presumption. The kind of unity that exists across various Eucharistic communities is a beautiful thing, because it represents the fullness of Christ to the outside world. Of course, it was not anyone's intention to rule out this unity completely; all they were saying was that it was not one of the features that necessarily constituted the Church, but it did belong to the Church's fullness, her *pleroma*, as they called it based on Paul, in which this is made visible to the outside world. But it is not exactly *necessary*, since one cannot add anything to the wholeness of Christ.

Starting from different premises, the Protestant notion of the Church pointed in the same direction. Luther, after all, had been unable to recognize the spirit of Christ in the universal Church amid the turmoil of his age; indeed, he viewed her as nothing less than the instrument of the

Antichrist. Nor did he consider the various Protestant national churches that were starting to become the new form of "Church" even in his lifetime to be the Church in the theological sense; he was realistic enough not to do that. It was quite apparent to him that the organizational structures given to these churches were little more than pragmatic apparatuses required by the social and political circumstances of the time, subject to the political powers in the absence of any other authority. The Church *qua* Church was not to be found in any of the larger institutions, neither in the universal Church of Catholicism nor in the Protestant regional churches that were being formed; as Luther saw it, the Church had withdrawn into the congregation, the assembly gathered to hear the Word of God where and when it is preached—it was they alone who were "Church". He likewise impressed this on his congregation in his choice of terminology, by making the word "church" a negative term and replacing it with "congregation" wherever he meant something positive. If you read Luther's translation of the Bible, you will see that in those places where the communion of Jesus Christ or its Old Testament prototypes are being referred to in a positive sense, the word "congregation" or "community" (*Gemeinde*) is used, whereas the word "Church" (*Kirche*) has a negative meaning.

Now, having explored these intervening thoughts, if we now turn our attention back to the conciliar text I read earlier, we will notice how certain nuances become evident that point to the internal tension in the text itself as it attempts to grapple with these questions. The council does not simply say that the Church is wholly present in every community that celebrates the Eucharist, but the way it formulates it (somewhat awkwardly when you first hear it, perhaps also hard to understand at first) is that the Church is truly present in all legitimate congregations of the faithful that, united with their shepherds are called churches. There are two important elements here that attest to the transformation, as it were, of the idea into this more narrow sense. The first is that the congregation must be legitimate for it to be the Church, and the proper response to the question of when congregations are legitimate is that they are legitimate when they are united with their shepherds. What does that mean? Are we just stuck with a kind of positivism where the institution asserts itself in its present form and forces its claims upon us, even though these claims do not follow theologically from such self-assertion? Or is it something even deeper? I will try to elucidate the text by asking you to consider the following points: First of all, what the council is trying to say is that no one can make himself the Church. A group cannot just meet up, read the New Testament together, and say, "now we are the Church, since the Lord is present wherever two or three are gathered in his name, after all." More than anything we do ourselves, it is the element of receiving that is essential to the character of the Church, just as faith comes from hearing and is not a product of our own decisions and reflections. Think about what we said earlier: The only option for us is to be redeemed, because the alternative would mean the radicalizing of our desire to be ourselves alone. This translates quite logically into the communal context—what comes first is the element of receiving, because faith comes from hearing and is not the product of a decision where we make ourselves into something. And this makes sense because, of course, faith is an encounter with that which I could never conceive of on my own or bring about through my own efforts; rather, it is something that has to come to *me*. This structure of receiving, of encountering, is what we call "sacrament".

And this is precisely why one of the most basic features of a sacrament is the fact that it is received and that no one administers it to himself. No one can baptize himself, since no one can make himself a Christian. No one can ordain himself a priest; no one can absolve himself of his own sins. And another consequence of this structure of encounter is that, given the inner logic of the structure of faith, perfect contrition and the overcoming of sin in oneself demands that a sacrament take the form of an encounter. And this is why, I should add, that when people pass the Eucharist around and administer to themselves, it is not just an offense against some rubric, but a misunderstanding and a violation of the structure of the sacrament itself. However, the fact that in this one sacrament, the priest can administer the sacred Gifts to himself points toward the *mysterium tremendum* to which he is exposed in the Eucharist: acting *in persona Christi*, simultaneously representing Christ *and* being a sinful human being that lives entirely on the reception of his grace. But we will come back to that later.

"Church" is not something we can make, but only something we can receive, and she has to be received from a source where she already, and truly, exists—from the sacramental communion of the Body of Christ as it makes its way through history. There is one more thing to add that should help us to understand what is meant by the difficult expression "legitimate congregations": Christ is whole everywhere, we said. That is the one very important point that the council articulated in common with our Orthodox brethren and with Protestant believers, and the full force of this truth is something that must be maintained. He is everywhere whole and not divided into pieces; he is also everywhere only one, and for this reason I can have the one Lord only in the unity that he himself is, in unity with the others who are also his Body and who are to become his Body ever anew in the Eucharist. Therefore, if there is to be a Eucharistic ecclesiology, then unity among congregations in the celebration of the Eucharist is not just an extrinsic addition to it, but is instead its intrinsic prerequisite. Only in unity is the One to be found, and if I go against unity, then I am always moving away from the One himself. In this respect, the council exhorts congregations to take responsibility for themselves and, by the same logic, rules out any notion of self-sufficiency. It sets forth an ecclesiology in which catholicity—that is, the fellowship of believers in all times and places—is not an extrinsic organizational feature but, rather, a grace that comes from within and at the same time a visible sign of the power of the Lord, who alone can provide unity across so many boundaries. So there we have this Eucharistic ecclesiology, which, on the one hand, involves each congregation exercising responsibility for itself but, at the same time, rules out self-sufficiency and demands that they exist within the whole.

## Unity and Collegiality

Now, very closely connected with this is the concept of episcopal collegiality, which, as everyone knows, was another of the principal pillars of the ecclesiology of Vatican II. This concept of collegiality of the bishops was likewise developed from the study of the liturgical structure of the Church, and it is a concept that I find to be very important, and just like with the issue of the local churches it is not just a matter of practical expediency—as if all we had to do was distribute the power a bit for things to run more smoothly— rather, it is first and foremost something that arises from the liturgical structure of the Church. If I remember correctly, the first person to formulate this idea clearly, thus opening the door for the council on this matter, was the Belgian liturgist Bernhard Botte. Indeed, I find it quite interesting that the Catholic encyclopedia *Lexikon für Theologie und Kirche*, first published in 1957, with the volume for "K" coming out in 1961, contains no entry for *Kollegialität*, collegiality. So you can see how around that time, even in the most advanced forms of German-language theology, the idea had not yet penetrated, had not yet become a term with which people were familiar. All the more important, then, to look into the genesis of this concept. Here, too, there is an important connection with the liturgical movement, which provided the fertile soil for almost all of the ideas we have explored thus far. Beyond its historical significance, this is important to note because it illustrates the deeper context of this idea, without which it cannot be properly understood.

The debate surrounding collegiality, as I have already hinted, is not a dispute over the relative share of power in the Church between the pope and the bishops, although of course it can easily degenerate into such a quarrel; and when that happens the parties involved should repeatedly ask themselves whether they have gone off track and are merely reenacting the infighting among the Apostles over who was the greatest. Nor is it primarily a dispute over juridical forms and institutional structures; rather, collegiality is by its very nature associated with *that* service which is really the true service performed by the Church in the first place, and that is the divine service, the liturgy. Botte took this idea from the oldest liturgical ordinances that have come down to us and developed his concept from there. During the council, this was frequently employed as an argument against opponents of collegiality, who believed it came from somewhere else. You see, many of them were unacquainted with this liturgical history but had studied law and were legal scholars who were familiar with the concept of collegiality in Roman law and Enlightenment law, where it is an expression for a kind of egalitarianism. So of course this led them to say that this was the Enlightenment being brought in through the back door, that this was a concept from a legal system that could not be reconciled with the law of the Church. In response to such claims, it was necessary to explain to them that our concept of collegiality comes neither from Roman law nor from Enlightenment law; it comes from the liturgical tradition of the Church. But then, of course, this also entails an obligation: if this is where the idea of collegiality comes from, then we can only properly understand it—and thus protect it from distortions—by constantly referring to this central point. So what does that mean, then?

Botte's research into the matter indicated that there were two levels to the concept of collegiality. At first these studies were of a purely historical nature, but it quickly became apparent how relevant they were to the present day. The first level of this idea, collegiality as a matter of simple historical record, consists of the fact that the bishop is surrounded by the *collegium* of the presbyters. This fact demonstrates that the notion of the individual congregations as self-sufficient entities was unknown in the ancient Church, since the presbyters who serve them are in fellowship with one another, and together they make up the bishop's "council". The congregations are held together by the presbyters, who are united around the bishop, and it is through the bishop that they are held within the wider unity of the universal Church. Hence, the priesthood always includes a kind of fellowship and affiliation with a bishop, who is in turn affiliated with the Church as a whole. This means, then, that the bishops, for their part, are not isolated, each of them acting on his own like a monarch in his own small kingdom, but that together they form, as the juridical language of the ancient Church puts it, the *ordo*, the order of bishops. This was taken from the contemporary language of Roman law, which divided society into several different *ordines*, or orders. Later, the word *ordo* was officially used to designate the sacrament of consecrating clergy; that is, holy orders. The significance of this is actually quite deep; for if the sacrament of consecration is called *ordo*, this means that an essential component of the sacrament of holy orders is entrance into a communal service, into the army of those who serve. The word *ordo*, moreover, tended to alternate with *collegium*. Both terms meant the same thing in the liturgical context: that the bishop is bishop, not on his own, but solely in the catholic communion of those bishops who came before him, who serve alongside him, and who will come after him. His ministry encompasses all of these dimensions, is rooted in the whole of the Church, in her "today" as well as in her openness to tomorrow. This word also entails the dimension of time: "Church" is not something we create today but something that we receive from the believers of history and that we pass on incomplete, to be fulfilled only at the Second Coming of the Lord. The council fused this with the other basic concept of the sacrament of episcopal consecration, the idea of apostolic succession, into an organic synthesis. This recalls the fact that, indeed, the Apostles, too, were a communion. Before they were called "apostles", which was probably not until after the Resurrection, they were referred to as "the Twelve". The Lord's calling of twelve men has a symbolic character that was understood by every Israelite, as it recalled the twelve sons of Jacob, from whom the Twelve Tribes that made up the people of Israel were descended. Twelve is therefore the symbolic number of the people of God. When Jesus calls twelve, this symbolic gesture is saying that he is himself the new Jacob-Israel and that with these men he is inaugurating a new people of God. Mark depicts this very clearly in his Gospel by describing the event of the calling with the words, "And he appointed twelve" (Mk 3:14). Moreover, everyone knew that twelve was also a cosmic number, the number of the signs of the zodiac that divide up the year, the time of man. This helps to underscore the unity of history and the cosmos, the cosmic character of salvation history. And it is important that we again make a connection to our earlier presentation here. The Church is not a human association formed on a lost planet somewhere but, rather, extends into the reality of creation. In the ultimate and definitive history of the universe, the Twelve are to be, as it were, the new "signs of the zodiac".

But now getting back to the matter that immediately concerns us, it is said that the Apostles are what they are only insofar as each is in the fellowship that is the communion of twelve, hence their numbers are replenished even after Judas' betrayal. Consequently, one becomes a successor of the Apostles by entering into the communion of those in whom their office continues. So, in this aspect as well, collegiality is thus an essential part of the episcopal office; it can be lived and exercised only in fellowship with those who at the same time represent the unity of the new people of God. Now if we ask ourselves what this means in practical terms, our first answer should be that it expressly emphasizes the catholic dimension of the episcopal office —that is, the communion of all bishops, yesterday, today, and tomorrow—and of priestly ordination and of everyday life in the congregation as well. Attempts to particularize, various forms of self-sufficiency, of isolation—all of these are fundamentally at odds with the idea of collegiality.

Collegiality, as articulated by the council, is not itself a juridical structure per se, though it is indeed a theological precept of the first order, as far as both the law of the Church and pastoral ministry are concerned. The juridical form that represents the most direct expression of the theological reality of collegiality is the ecumenical council. Hence, in the new Code of Canon Law, the ecumenical council is one of the only other things discussed in the article that specifically deals with the college of bishops. All other applications of collegiality, such as the bishops' conferences, the various episcopal councils, and so on, are internal analogues, attempts to put it into concrete terms, but cannot be derived from it directly; rather, they are approaches to, means, or methods of secondary mediation of this great fundamental principle in the day-to-day reality of life. They should always be measured by the extent to which they correspond to the basic substance with which we are dealing here: transcending the local horizon and entering into the shared experience of Catholic unity, which has always included the dimension of the history of the faith from the beginning until the Second Coming of the Lord.

## Church as People of God

One last step: In our discussion of the idea of collegiality, we finally came across a phrase you have probably all been waiting to hear, and that is the idea of the Church as "people of God". So what is it all about? Again, in order to get a proper understanding here, we are going to have to go back to take a brief look at the developments that preceded the council. After the initial enthusiasm surrounding the development of the concept of the Body of Christ, it was gradually followed by even deeper explorations of the idea and corrections along two lines. I have already attempted to explain the first of these corrections—it can be found particularly in the works of Henri de Lubac, who took the, let us say, rather inspired but mostly unstructured idea of the Mystical Body of Christ and gave it a concrete form in the *communio* ecclesiology, thus opening it up to questions about the Church's juridical order and the relationship of the local church to the universal Church. The other kind of correction began in the late 1930s in Germany, where various theologians observed critically that the idea of the Mystical Body of Christ ultimately did not do enough to clarify the relationship between the visible and the invisible, law and grace, order and life. And so they suggested the concept of the "people of God", which is found primarily in the Old Testament, as a more comprehensive way of describing the Church, one that would incidentally also be easier to convey in sociological and juridical terms, whereas "Body of Christ" remains an image that, though important, does not quite satisfy theology's demand for conceptualization. This was also an epistemological critique more than anything else, the claim of which was that theology was supposed to arrive at concepts, that it must not remain at the level of images, that this cannot be the final stage of reflection. "People of God", on the other hand, can be understood as a concept, which then transcends and integrates these images as well. I would say, however, that this last criticism is, in a certain sense, a superficial one, since it proceeds too much from a general ideal in theology that takes conceptualization as its supreme standard. Nevertheless, the approach was made and given in order to be taken farther.

These initial criticisms gradually led to the development of the positive content with which the concept of the people of God then entered into the council's ecclesiology. One of the first major points where the physiognomy of the "people of God" concept began to take shape was the controversy over Church membership that had developed in connection with the encyclical *Mystici corporis Christi* (The Mystical Body of Christ), promulgated by Pius XII in 1943. Pius XII had stated that Church membership was dependent on three conditions: baptism, right belief, and affiliation with the juridical unity of the Church. Defined in this way—and, indeed, this certainly corresponds to a very ancient tradition that membership in the Church is based solely on these three things: sacrament, faith, and concrete communion with the Church as represented by the communion of the bishops and the pope—then while this initially makes sense when viewed from inside the Catholic sphere, the grave consequence was that it meant non-Catholics were completely excluded from membership in the Church. And this point was inevitably met with serious repercussions in Germany in particular, simply because the ecumenical question is so urgent there that people were unable to find reassurance in the statement; nor were they willing to, especially since the Code of Canon Law at the time offered another perspective, the canon law tradition itself, according to which baptism, even on its own, established a form of inalienable affiliation with the Church. In the face of these two traditions, the more narrow dogmatic one articulated by Pius XII in his encyclical and the more wide-ranging one recorded in canon law, people began to wonder whether the image of the Mystical Body was perhaps too narrow a point of departure to define the manifold forms of affiliation with the Church that actually do exist now in the complexity of human history.

The image of the Body provides only one notion of affiliation, that of the "member", where one is either a member or not—there are no intermediate stages. But, people
asked, is not the point of departure implied by this image
too narrow, since there obviously *are* intermediate stages? It
was in this aporia that they came across the concept of the
"people of God", which was without a doubt more wide-
ranging and more flexible, and it was precisely this usage
of the term that the council adopted in the Constitution
on the Church. The second chapter, which is titled "On
the People of God", deals with this question and, thus, uti-
lizes the "people of God" image because it makes it possible
to describe the relation of non-Catholic Christians to the
Catholic Church by saying that they are "joined" to her,
and that of non-Christians by saying that they are "related
to" her, and both instances are included in the general idea
of the people of God.

We can therefore say that the concept of the "people of
God" was introduced by the council primarily as a way of
returning to the project of ecumenism, and this is true in
another respect as well, for the rediscovery of the Church
after the First World War started out as a phenomenon
that was common to Catholics and Protestants alike. I recall that at around the same time as Guardini was coming
up with his "Church coming to life in the souls of men",
Otto Dibelius, who was then Evangelical [Lutheran] Bishop
of Berlin, spoke of the "beginning of the century of the
Church". The liturgical movement, too, was by no means
restricted to the Catholic Church. But the very fact that
they had grown together also gave rise to criticism on both
sides. The concept of the Body of Christ was developed
in the Catholic Church to the point that some theologians
would say that the Church was the continuation of Christ's

life on earth, describing the Church as the ongoing Incarnation of the Son that would continue till the end of time.
This, however, elicited opposition from Protestants, who
saw in this an intolerable self-identification of the Church
with Christ, in which the Church was worshipping herself
by making herself Christ and setting herself up as infallible.

Similarly, though without going quite so far, Catholic
thinkers also began to find that this formulation ascribed a
definitive character to all the official acts and utterances of
the Church that made it appear as though every criticism
was an attack on Christ himself and simply overlooked the
human, all too human, aspects of the Church. They insisted
that it was once again necessary to emphasize the Christological difference clearly, that the Church is not identical
with Christ, but stands in relation to him. It is a Church of
sinners that is in constant need of purification and renewal,
that is always in a state of *becoming* the Church. Thus, the
idea of reform became a crucial element of the "people of
God" concept, one that could not be derived in the same
way from the idea of the Body of Christ. This second aspect was very important to the council as well. In addition
to these, there was also a third aspect that played a role
in promoting the concept of the people of God. In 1939,
Tübingen-based Protestant exegete Ernst Käsemann wrote
a monograph on the Letter to the Hebrews titled *The Wan-
dering People of God*. In the context of the ideas discussed by
the council, this title became something of a slogan, as it
gave voice to something that was becoming more and more
evident in the course of the struggle to draft the Constitution on the Church: The Church has not yet reached her
destination; her true hope still lies ahead of her, and the
eschatological import of the concept of the Church is now
clear. Most importantly, however, this made it possible to

declare the unity of salvation history, which encompasses both Israel and the Church together on their way of pilgrimage. It thus became possible to express the historic nature of the Church, which is on her way and will become herself entirely only when she has walked the paths down through the ages, ending in God's hands.

# Unity and Pluralism

In our final lecture, we are going to be considering a variety of different topics. For while I felt it was necessary to dedicate at least some time to discussing the Magisterium, I also did not want just to make it the topic of its own lecture, if only because I did not want to give anyone the impression that I meant to equate the actions of the Magisterium as such with those of God. This gave me the idea of approaching the issue from a different direction, namely by asking the question: "In what way can there be pluralism, plurality in the Church, and how might we relate this to unity?" In developing my response to this question, however, I would like to start with a brief history of the idea of pluralism starting with its origins outside the Church, what it initially meant quite independently of theology, as this, I believe, will also make it easier to understand the theological content of the concept as it is used within the Church. And finally, so as to kill several birds with one stone, I thought I might find a way to relate the whole thing to the topic printed on the conference program: "Living with the Church". What does that mean? And how does it work, in concrete terms? Of course, we are only going to be able to touch briefly on each of these issues.

## The History of Pluralism as an Idea

So, the question we were asking was, "What does pluralism mean, originally; where does the idea of pluralism come from?" As far as I am aware, the term itself was developed around the turn of the twentieth century in England for use in the political-social sphere. It was proposed in opposition to a certain doctrine of sovereignty that saw the individual as the only entity standing in the way of the state and its claim to authority and in which the state's claim to authority was, of course, quite far-reaching. In contrast to this idea, pluralism seeks to relativize the state's claim. The concept is based on the observation that each individual lives within a variety of communities that exist prior to the state, in a variety of social groupings, from which follow a variety of social roles, none of which is quite capable of absorbing the human person entirely. From this point of view, the state is just one grouping among a number of others; it cannot exercise ultimate authority over the individual, but can only lay claim to him in a particular social role, alongside of which there are various other roles. The network of concurrent and competing roles is thus conceived of as an order of freedom. At all times, there is more to man than the individual role that he occupies; at no point can he be totally subsumed. The multiplicity of groups that uphold this order and play a part in the shaping of social life act, on the one hand, to ensure order against anarchy, but, on the other hand and at the same time, they also constitute a safeguard against the concentration of power and are supposed to guarantee latitude for the individual personality. Such ideas, which were decidedly contrary to Enlightenment ideas regarding the state—and this, I think, is really interesting and quite important for our purposes—had arisen in connection with studies on the cooperative system of the Middle Ages; that is, by hearkening back to pre-Enlightenment Christian conceptions of the state. In that respect, it can be said that this original idea of pluralism is thoroughly in line with the social and political traditions of Christendom. Apart from all this, Catholic social teaching had also been developing similar lines of thought since the nineteenth century. The restriction of state authority to its proper domain, along with the emphasis on social units that are prior to the state, is one of the oldest constants of Christian efforts to establish the proper form of the polity.

Of course, given the inner logic of the ideas of the thinkers to whom we are referring here, they were bound to become an issue for the Church one day as well. If every corporate social entity is merely relative, and the Church herself asserts this in her very struggle with the state; if every social entity may demand obedience only within its legitimate sphere and the social role associated with it, does this not then apply to the Church as well? Does this not necessarily mean that the Church, too, ought to be seen as one association among many, possessing correspondingly limited authority? Does it not follow that the conscience, the ultimate and most intimate part of the personality that exists above all social roles, should be considered inviolable and off-limits to the Church as well? Should the Church not restrict herself to the sphere of interests appointed to her and seeing to people's religious needs? This is the question that even today thoroughly defines the struggle over which form the Church's claim to authority should take, with regard to both the state and the individual. However, this also raises the opposite question for the Church: What is, in fact, a religious need, a religious interest? Is it a narrowly circumscribed need alongside other needs, like the need for clothing, for recreation, for professional fulfillment, and so on? Or is it not that religious need is precisely the expression of man's ultimate and essential bond, in which it is no longer a question of this or that social role, but one centered entirely on man himself? And then, in consequence, is the community not dedicated to fulfilling this ultimate need, on which man's finding of his identity thereby depends, *ipso facto* also the true locus of man's identity, in which he transcends all roles? Where else and how else is he to transcend them at all and then, somewhere and at some point, still be himself in all his roles? And is it not therefore necessary for the community dedicated to the fulfillment of this need to be wholly different in kind from all other communities? The questions that emanated from this debate at the beginning of the century at first made little impact in Central Europe, where, in the period between the two world wars, the intellectual climate to which I alluded in my previous lecture was dominated by a new interest in the idea of authority. In the 1920s, Carl Schmitt, who had recently created his "political theology", criticized the ideas associated with pluralism as subversive, receiving widespread agreement among his contemporaries. Only after the egregious abuse of authority in the authoritarian behavior of the totalitarian systems did a new situation finally emerge here in Central Europe. The image of society that developed in Germany and all over Central Europe after the war now corresponded to the pluralistic model. Both in terms of their legal status and social role, the churches became a kind of voluntary association. This was, and still is, the societal form that enabled them to assert their freedom and develop their autonomy with respect to the state.

## The Uniformization of Man

Now, while more questions might be raised here concerning matters both internal and external, I am going to put them aside so that we can immediately proceed to the next step in our reflections. To wit, if we look at the intellectual landscape of the period we have been discussing, we have this one movement, namely, the breaking down of the state in favor of various social institutions that exist prior to the state, whereby a certain preponderance is given to these institutions vis-à-vis the state, leading to a great emphasis on the pluralism of roles and forms. Yet there are also certain currents running in the opposite direction, as, side by side with the pursuit of pluralism, the modern world has likewise been subjected to an increasingly powerful movement toward uniformity, with the emergence of ever greater political and economic consolidation, together with the concentrations of power that this entails. The mass media have brought about a kind of uniformity in thought, speech, and behavior that would have been unimaginable in earlier periods. Very specific images, very specific forms of behavior make their way into every last corner of the world. Right down to the gestures and the vocabulary he uses, man is, so to speak, molded into a certain template, his speech and actions increasingly made up of prefabricated components, as it were.

This "uniformization" of man is drastically noticeable, especially if one travels around the world a bit. This tendency toward uniformity now shapes man from the outside in, reaching down to his unconscious, down into his dreams —there really is some truth to the idea of the "dream factory", it seems. Anyway, this uniformization is the result of the level of communication previously achieved during the technological reshaping of the world, which itself was based on the use of math to decode nature. All great philosophies, whether you think of Plato, Aristotle, Neoplatonism, the various forms of medieval philosophy, the modern era—

they all retain their cultural particularity. Aristotle was only able to speak the way he did because he lived in the Greece of that time, and the way Kant speaks is just how someone in East Prussia spoke back then, and not as he would have had he lived in France. So, while philosophy has been able to achieve a level of influence far beyond its place of origin, there still remains—even in those areas where philosophy makes great advances in its consideration of universal truth —the particularity of each individual language.

In contrast to this, science and technological civilization are almost entirely devoid of cultural peculiarity. A mathematical formula is the same everywhere, and then, with only minor variations, the technical applications of a given formula are likewise essentially the same everywhere as well. This uniformity, which thus emerges in the world as a result of technology and the principles behind it, is possible only because technological civilization limits itself to one sector of reality as recognized by man. It is inherently positivistic, encompassing only that section of reality as a whole that can be subjected to the positivist method. We are all familiar with how much can be achieved by this approach. We experience it on a daily basis and live with it in the familiar aspects of our ordinary lives, up to the very use of this microphone right here.

It is slowly beginning to dawn on us how high the purchase price of all of this is; we can sense it in the subterranean rumbling of the being that is man; indeed, of the earth on which we live and of the air that we breathe. Now, in speaking about the "purchase price" here, I am thinking not so much of the necessary double-edged nature of every action, but of the deeper issue at play here, which we also talked about in our previous lecture. The confinement of knowledge to that which can be observed—going by the literal meaning of the word, what we can "hold in front of" us—and thus to what we can put in front of our faces and hold in our hands requires that we forgo any actual assessment of value, indeed, that we forgo the question of truth in general. What are things beyond their functioning? What am I, who am I? I am not claiming that this method would have to exclude such knowledge per se; perhaps it could very well occur in its proper place, but in its actual course this does not happen. Because this course is, so to speak, the path of success, which everybody can see and the one by which we also live, it is tempting to draw the erroneous conclusion that only that which is deemed to be certain in this way is reasonable, and only that which is recognized as reasonable in this sense has the right to exist.

## Philosophy and Truth

So I repeat, it is not the method as such but, rather, the overpowering nature of its success that threatens to bring about the destruction of man. This explains, first of all, how this uniformization of technological civilization has led to the fragmentation of philosophical consciousness and the dissolution of its actual content—namely, the question of truth, which now appears unscientific. So the situation in which we find ourselves is one where, on the one hand, the question of truth has become "unscientific" and hardly anyone dares ask it anymore, yet, on the other hand, it is something mankind does truly need. Now, there are two ways out of this situation, though in reality they are really but one. Philosophy is man's attempt to look beyond all particulars and ask: "Who am I, and what ought I to do?" Attempting to assert itself, philosophy, especially in the form of analytic philosophy, may try to satisfy completely all the requirements of the positivist method. Yet it has ceased to be philosophy when, in doing this, the question of truth, the question that once brought forth the university in the first place, is dismissed as "unscientific" in its own domain and thus, effectively, in society at large.

But because pure positivism is unlivable over the long term, it becomes necessary to find another way out, and I think that the student uprisings of 1968—even if I do not at all approve of their content or the form they took—were a wholly necessary revolt against this kind of positivism, with which it is indeed impossible to live. Things were such that something was going to have to give eventually, but when the time came, the way out was to assert that truth is not the measure of man but a product of man. Truth is replaced by empirical confirmation; it can now be produced "scientifically"; it lies in the *praxis* that brings forth the future. The resulting situation for the individual Christian was described by Munich psychologist Albert Görres—quite aptly, I think: The Christian who lives at this time necessarily thinks in its terms, telling himself that he has selected the cocktail of plausibilities that tastes best to him. Christians who are secure in their faith often come across to themselves and to others as overbearing or megalomaniacal, afflicted with an infallibility complex.

Once pluralism is understood in these terms, the idea of a magisterial teaching authority becomes pure absurdity and utter presumption. I am convinced that the vehemence with which every kind of magisterial intervention is fought these days is based to a large extent on this mindset. The claim to be able to proclaim the truth as a universal and thus binding quantity comes across as abstruse medieval arrogance. Very late in his life, Guardini also had something very interesting to say about this. On his eightieth birthday, he once again gave a short speech at the university on irony in Plato, in which he noted how peculiar it was that wherever Plato talks about those things that are most profound, what he considers to be the truth and thus wishes to communicate to man, he uses irony—or what we in Bavaria might call *Gaudi*, or good fun; that he casts himself in a ridiculous light, to where one might think that he is only playing around. Guardini says that this is in fact Plato's profound way of doing justice to the situation in which man finds himself, where, on the one hand, he must hold fast to the truth and never forget that he has been given the capacity to know the truth, but, at the same time, he has to accept that when he speaks the truth he is, so to speak, like a fool and must keep a certain degree of ironic distance from it by accepting his own folly without allowing the truth to become entirely lost in it.

## Theology and Pluralism

But that does not cover the full panorama of problems that we open up by doing this. Up to now, you see, I have been talking about the domain of the state, the domain where authority is formed and where pluralism takes hold. Then the deeper level of the fundamental human question of truth, as it is meant to be represented by philosophy, resulted in this view whereby the idea of a teaching authority seems somehow absurd in the present situation. But now that I have spoken about the crisis of science and philosophy, one more question remains: "What about theology?" Once again, I have found Guardini's autobiographical notes to be significant and quite reliable when it comes to shedding light on this problem. He describes the difficult time he had being

promoted to an academic teaching position, and what made
it so difficult was the fact that the field of theology in Germany had fully submitted itself to the methodological canon
of the university. As a university discipline, it naturally did
not wish to lag behind the others when it came to scholarly and scientific reputation. But in the German universities of those days, there were only two areas of scholarship
that were considered truly scientific and thus appropriate
for academic study at the university, precisely because they
seemed to adhere to this "safety protocol" of positivity:
namely, history and the natural sciences. So what, then, is
a theology faculty to do if it wants to be able to keep up?
The way out was relatively simple: theology cannot become
a natural science, of course, but it can become history, since
it does in fact have a long history. And this is how academic
theology ended up becoming reduced to historical theology.
The situation was essentially no different when I completed
my doctorate: you may have heard other things discussed
in the lecture hall, but—and I even think this is right, in
principle—a doctoral dissertation simply had to be historical in nature if it was going to be considered serious scholarship. So that is how it was back then, and it was probably
even more so in the period after the Second World War.
But this ran afoul of Guardini's whole genius, contradicting
the way his intellect was structured at its core, for he had
absolutely no interest in history. He was not at all interested
in what one person or another once said about this or that;
rather, he was only interested in the *how* of things. He did
not want to write about something thought up by someone
else at some point, but wanted to know what is true and
what matters concern us. But of course he was not going to
get a dissertation topic by pursuing these goals, nor would
they allow him to penetrate the field of academic theology,

as none of the things that interested him fell within the scope of the kind of theology that led to a doctorate. He eventually succeeded, albeit with some drudgery, to write a historical thesis after all, but he still felt it was contrary to what he wanted to do. He then describes that even in Berlin, where he finally ended up becoming a professor, but was rejected by the university, he felt, he knew, that this canon of methods was really not for him, but that what he was doing was nevertheless still worthy of study at the university. If not at the present university, he thought, he was working for a future university that would one day exist. I do not think it exists even today, but at the same time I believe that Guardini was right and that it ought to.

Now, compared to the kind of theology that was practiced in the twenties, where Guardini had to find his own way, things are quite different now. Historical theology still exists, it is an important field, and I personally love it very much, but it is obvious that it in no way covers the whole of theology. Theology has to be able to assist in the care of souls, the preaching of the Gospel—that is ultimately what it is there for. And when it comes to these things, it is not necessary to explain what this or that was like at one time, but only necessary to answer the questions asked by man in today's world —what is the right way for him to live his life and respond to the will of God today? So we know that history alone cannot account for everything theology has to offer, and this is the point where the situation of the late sixties comes along and brings about something new: namely, the reorientation of the idea of truth toward praxis. We no longer ask about what has been, but we also no longer ask about the unattainable truth, because there is none, and things are not rational anyway. Instead, it is we who create the truth by building a more humane world. The reorientation of the idea of truth toward praxis, which originated in the neo-Marxist movement, called the old positivism of the university thoroughly into question. This appeared to be the long-hoped-for opportunity for theology to achieve a new status in the university and, thus, renewed relevance in society at large. Because now there was no need to disregard the issue of truth, but nor was there a need to continue with the futile, nonscientific business of finding it in the voice of being or in Scripture; theology was now concerned with producing truth by means of methodological praxis.

Now, so-called "practical theology" provided the starting point and the end point of everything within the whole array of theological subjects. The entire edifice of theology as an academic discipline, so it seemed, could be understood from the point of view of practical theology, part of an effort to bring about a more humane future on the basis of memories preserved in the history of faith. This concept—that practical theology, in its aim to produce a more humane future, also makes use of human experiences that are preserved in faith (which the other theological disciplines could then dwell on)—seemed to reinvigorate theology with a sense of purpose, making it a thoroughly "scientific" field once more in the most contemporary sense of the term, one that was entirely real and practical. Needless to say, this was an exciting prospect and an exciting moment for theology, particularly in Germany. I believe it is only when one understands this situation to some degree that one can begin to make sense of how seemingly all at once—and this is something I experienced for myself in Tübingen—theologians and their communities became the most effective proponents of the neo-Marxist movement. It also makes it easier to understand the passion with which the scientific character and the consequent indispensability of Marxist analysis was invoked. For if it were not scientific, then of course this whole opportunity would collapse.

There is an interesting paradox here. It was only Marxism, at least in this particular situation, people thought, that could help the ailing field of theology back onto its feet and give it back its self-confidence as a true academic discipline. And it was only an influx of religious passion that could restore in Marxism, already scientifically and politically depleted outside of those areas where it still held sway, the splendor of hope for humanity. It is at this point that we are once again confronted with the problem of pluralism. The concept of a theology in which truth has been superseded by praxis makes no provision for pluralism at the time when it reaches its true goal, as little as the Marxist conception itself does, in fact. One liberation theologian recently added to the functions of Church unity enumerated in the letter to the Ephesians, "one Lord, one faith, one baptism, one God and Father of us all" (Eph 4:5–6). He said that they should add "one option", by which he meant a political option, and that this option, inasmuch as it is unity in praxis, is the only real unity. Pluralism has its role as an intermediate stage and only as an intermediate stage. As long as the ecclesial theology that is defined by the Creed remains in place, pluralism is needed in order to create space for theology oriented toward praxis. In the end, however, there can be only *one* option, which means only *one* praxis and, consequently, ultimately only *one* theory at the service of this praxis. In other words, the final result of relinquishing the truth is not liberation, but uniformity.

## Faith and Social Action

Now we can see something like a preliminary thesis beginning to emerge from the things I have been saying, which
I would like to articulate here. I might put it something
like this: From the very beginning, it has been a constitutive element of the Christian faith to seek to lead man to
his ultimate bond, his bond to the truth. This is the distinguishing feature of the kind of relationship that comes from
faith. Because faith is concerned with man's bond with the
truth, it offers liberation in those areas that lie farther in
the foreground of his existence. This is where the connection to the political/social model of pluralism developed at
the beginning comes in. Faith guides and directs man at the
deepest level, but it does not prescribe to him his individual
social roles. This is why the Church is not a state and why
those who are Christian can live in a diverse range of gov-
ernmental systems and a variety of social groupings. This is
not meant to imply freedom from obligation, and Christians
cannot retreat into mere interiority or forsake their social
responsibilities. Faith is indeed an "option", one with a very
definite shape provided by the Decalogue as interpreted in
light of the New Testament. It is an option for equal rights
for all people and thus for the inviolability of those rights
by power. It is an option for the unconditional authority of
truth and man's bond to truth. It is an option for marital
fidelity and for the family as the fundamental unit of society. It is an option for the inviolability of human life and
for the right to life. From the very beginning it has been
an option for the disenfranchised and the oppressed, or, as
the Bible puts it, for the widows, orphans, and foreigners.
In this respect, the faith does indeed contain unambiguous
political and social imperatives that will frequently bring

Christians and the Church into conflict with the powers that be, and a conception of the Christian faith where martyrdom is no longer a possibility, where everything is so perfectly balanced that there is no more need to expect any difficulties, is one that is simply no longer faithful to the Crucified One. The faith does entail clear political and social imperatives that will frequently put it in conflict with the powers that be, but, at the same time, it has to be said that this does not make it a recipe for political action, and therefore the Church cannot and must not become a political party. Because she must fundamentally deny the totalizing claim of the political realm, she is also opposed to every analysis that claims to be the one possible and, thus, the only sure way to bring about a healthy society. Such an ostensibly "scientific" approach is necessarily unscientific, as it presupposes that man can be treated as if he were a mechanism and because it also presupposes a physics of man whereby even his physical body can be engineered with certainty, a physics of man that does not exist. If it did, then man would no longer be man, but a machine. Pluralism in the interactions between Church, politics, and society is therefore a constitutive element of Christianity, yet without implying a kind of relativism. These two things need to remain in balance. This pluralism is the result of the approach taken by Christianity, a product of the Christian option, because Christianity teaches that all actual manifestations of politics and society are relative; this, in turn, shifts theocracy, the rule of God, into the eschaton, which is not brought about by our efforts, but which merely serves as the guiding measure toward which we live. Consequently, the Church must be skeptical of all political and social monocultures. The freedom to choose from a variety of political and social options is in the interest of faith itself, just as the distinction between Church and state, the freedom to form various communities within a given state, and, thus, religious liberty all spring from faith's very essence. Of course, there may be situations—once again, lest anyone accuse me of advocating passivity—that make it necessary for Christians to come together in order to engage in political action, such as when one or more of the basic options that I mentioned are at stake. But such instances are temporary, and the particular association in question is not thereby given a general and permanent mandate of the Church. Moreover, the form taken by such action-oriented unity must be situated within the political sphere and cannot be prescribed by the Church, neither by the hierarchy nor by any "grassroots" movement.

So with this in mind, the thesis I have been working toward would go like this: Because faith represents an ultimate bond to God, who is Truth, it provides man with norms for concrete social action within the social order, yet it is not in social or political praxis that the community of believers finds unity, but only in the truly binding nature of the truth itself. Where these bonds are dissolved for the sake of perceived freedom, new constraints arise in their place, because then it becomes necessary to establish other bonds, which are then actually self-made. The line from John's Gospel, "The truth will make you free" [Jn 8:32] is clearly true in an empirical sense as well: The bond to truth liberates politics from sacral bonds. To this effect, not only is pluralism compatible with faith; it is proper to it, and, to a certain degree, which can change according to the situation, it is even necessary.

Well, that is the question as it is posed from the outside, in the area of the Church's external relations, so to speak. In the second part, we will have to turn our question inward and ask: How does this actually work within the Church? Could it be that the monism of Magisterium and dogma really are all that there is?

This is a very broad topic, and I had planned to look at only two specific aspects of it, namely, that of the "universal church and particular churches" and "theology and theologies". However, I am going to leave some things out in order to focus our discussion on the specific problem of the episcopacy and papal primacy, now that we have already considered some of the more general issues at play in the previous lecture.

## Episcopacy and Primacy

I believe that the relationship between the episcopacy and the primacy of the pope conceals a more fundamental principle of the Church's constitution that is of great importance to her essential nature and to the form taken by Christian communities in general; namely, the cooperation between the personal and the communal principle. Monocracy, rule by one person alone, is always dangerous. Even when the person in question acts out of a high level of moral responsibility, he can still get lost in unilateral thinking or become rigid. It is for this reason that the evolution of constitutions in the modern era has generally worked more and more toward collegial bodies and the reciprocal checks inherent to them. This has brought about many positive things— we experience them in our democracies—but we are also now witnessing situations in which the limits and the dangers of these kinds of constitutional structures, where responsibility slips into anonymity, are becoming apparent. In the end, no one person has to account for what has been done, because it is the group that has decided, to which no one considers himself wholly identical. The group spreads out the responsibility for decisions and takes them out of the hands of individuals; majorities are products of chance and are ultimately not capable of bearing responsibility for themselves in the legal sense. It is precisely because it recognizes this that the constitution of the Church provides for the harmonious interplay between the communal principle and the principle of personal responsibility at all levels, even if the juridical character varies quite widely from case to case. I believe that this interplay is the characteristic feature of the Church's communal structure in general and an essential part of it. Let me suggest just a few of the different levels here: the pastor is joined to his congregation, the bishop to his presbytery and his fellow bishops, the pope to the communion of bishops. At the same time, however, there is an ultimate personal responsibility that cannot be revoked, substituted, or dissolved into any kind of collective, whether at the level of the parish, the diocese, or the universal Church. The structure of the Church's constitution that people used to call—incorrectly, I believe—the "monarchical episcopate" should more correctly be called the "principle of personal responsibility" in the Church. It is in persons that the Church is made tangible and may be held accountable. These persons cannot arbitrarily decide things as they see fit, but must do so by binding their conscience to the faith of the universal Church and by listening to those who are under their care.

As a communion, the Church can and must allow herself to make use of conscience in her constitution in order to establish a bond between the community as a whole and the individual person. Papal primacy loses any sense of place or actual substance if it is the sole exception, if it has no counterpart among the preceding levels—the personal responsibility of a bishop, which he cannot delegate to any group, or the different form of personal responsibility of the parish priest. Conversely, the episcopal principle amounts to nothing if there is not anything at the level of the universal Church that corresponds to its significance for the particular church. It is precisely this personalist approach to authority and responsibility that gives rise to a variegated and vibrant pluralism. The college of bishops is a body that is made up of those who bear the ultimate responsibility for the particular church, which is itself wholly Church, and in which they embody the responsibility of the universal Church. This alone is what gives the college of bishops its vital power as a group, reflecting the diversity of the Spirit in the one Church.

But there is also a peculiar antagonism between the two movements. At first, it does appear that if the papacy is indeed the guarantor of unity, then each particular church really is the one Church. But viewed historically, and this is something that has not received enough consideration, the coexistence of systems and structures pertaining to the particular church and those of the universal Church in all dioceses has already shown itself to be an engine of pluralism. I will cite just one example of this: the Mendicant Controversy of the thirteenth century. The situation up to that point was such that the traditional form of monasticism had become seamlessly integrated into the episcopal order of the Church, as the individual monasteries typically confined themselves to their own territory and did not intervene in the actual apostolic work of pastoral ministry. But now, with the rise of the mendicant orders, new pastoral movements were beginning to crop up, dynamically spreading out from a central location and providing preaching and

penitential services all across the continent; this placed them
in direct competition with ordinary pastoral work. The strife
between the secular clergy and the mendicant orders in the
universities is also a sign of the broader struggle to break
out of the feudal order into modernity toward more versatile
reforms of economic life, and in this sense, it represented
a clash between different historical eras. In this dispute, as
in all human conflicts, neither side is completely right on
its own, but each is right *and* wrong in its own way. But
it is certainly true that the mendicant orders created a new,
dynamic way of proclaiming the Gospel in a system that was
becoming rigid and ossified, that they brought with them a
new means of making the universal Church as such tangible and actively present as a living reality in the individual
local churches, and that it was only by this means that the
universal Church became capable of acting as the universal Church, thus becoming a missionary Church once more.
Pluralism in the form of dynamic apostolic activity provided
by a movement rooted in the universal Church as a second
force alongside the more homegrown pastoral ministry of
the local church has proved to be a fruitful state of affairs.

But this universal-Church activity in the local church and
thus its contribution to a pluralistic and, ultimately, unifying
form of pastoral care was made possible only by its connection to a concrete and theologically grounded institution of
the universal Church, the Petrine Office. Such a thing is not
to be found anywhere else, nor can it be. It seems to be that,
up to now, far too little notice has been given to the fact
that the two great impetuses behind the development of the
doctrine of papal primacy and the office of the primate to its
full form in the first place came about not so much due to an
interest in unity, but in response to the demands of pluralism. The primacy as it exists today has been shaped by two

major impetuses: the first is the conflict over the freedom of the Church in the West; that is, over the distinction between church and state. The only reason they were able to achieve this freedom is precisely because the Western Church was not just one particular church, but a living organ of the universal Church, and everywhere on earth, membership in this universal Church required separation from the state and prevented the formation of state churches, where the state is identified with the Church. The emblematic figure of this impetus was Gregory VII. The emergence of the non-identity between church and state, the fundamental plurality on which the Church's distinctiveness rests, was driven by this institution of unity. And the other impetus is indeed the one provided by the "grassroots" movements that arose in the universal Church, which is what one would have to call the religious movements of the thirteenth century, in which the apostolic dynamism of the universal Church enriched and supplemented pastoral ministry at the local level.

As I see it, the two circumstances that gave the primacy its current form are something like a verification of the Petrine Office arising from the praxis and the experience of the Church throughout her history, and both are still of utmost importance. For even today, and today more than ever, only the Petrine Office, the reality of the universal Church, is capable of safeguarding the distinction between the particular church and the state or society that surrounds it. Likewise, today we are also once again experiencing the phenomenon of "bottom-up" movements that transcend locality, in which new charisms burst forth and breathe life into pastoral ministry at the local level. As in the past, such movements that cannot be directly attributed to the principle of the episcopacy find their theological and practical support in the primacy, which thus continues to promote

a vibrant and fruitful pluralism in the Church precisely because it makes ecclesial unity a concrete reality and not an
abstract principle.

So much, then, for the question of "Episcopacy and Primacy"; now let us continue with the question of "Theology and Theologies".

## *"Hinduization of Christianity"?*

The questions about the structure of the Church that we
briefly touched upon necessarily point to the content that
those structures exist to serve. Until recently, it seemed as
though this content, or at least the essential core of it, was
clearly defined in the Creeds, the decrees of the Church
councils, and the dogmas of the Church. Today this essential core has itself come under discussion. Though it is general practice not to call dogma itself into question, many
do point out the cultural contingency of all human speech.
Faith, they say, cannot be passed down in definitive formulas; rather, we must always find new ways of expressing it.

Now before we go on, I would like to give the floor again
to Albert Görres, who once spoke of a "Hinduization of
Christianity". "Hinduization", he explained, happens when
we are concerned, no longer with the propositions of the
faith, but with the experience of contact with a spiritual
atmosphere that leads beyond all things that can be said. By
way of contrast, Görres described the historical physiognomy of Christianity in no uncertain terms: There is no
Christianity without a tendency toward concision, there is
no teaching of Jesus without a skeleton, without a dogmatic
principle behind it. Jesus had no intention of bringing about
an emotional movement devoid of real content; his message

is a particular one, and he does not agree with everyone. Catholic Christians believe that there are vitally necessary contours to the faith, without which it would become meaningless. They believe that the Church can and should see to it that these contours are "catholic" in the original sense of the word, that is, that they manifest at all times the whole of revelation, unrestricted and undistorted—so says Görres. As a matter of fact, I believe that faith heals and strengthens inasmuch as it opens man up to knowledge that is true; for otherwise it is not knowledge. It tells him what he himself might be able to sense from afar, but of which no human being could truly assure him, the truth about the reason and the purpose of his own existence. It gives him the knowledge that alone makes all other knowledge meaningful, because it tells him the Why and the Wherefore. To remove from faith its claim to truth, and stated, understandable truth at that, would be an example of the kind of false modesty that is the direct opposite of humility, because rather than accepting the *conditio humana*, it renounces it; because it renounces the dignity of being human, which is what makes its sufferings bearable and makes man great. If we accept this, then it follows that it has specific content, with identifiable reference points that we can name. It means that even the simple—and them especially—can have proper faith and not just a faith for the less mentally sophisticated; they can believe rightly and truly, in every age. If it is necessary for faith to be able to present the essentials of the faith without distortion, then there must be an authority that is able to do this, then the Church herself must have a voice; she must be able to express herself as the Church. This implies that faith and theology are not the same thing. They each have their own voice, but the voice of theology is dependent on that of faith and oriented toward it. It is interpretation, and that is what it must remain. When it no longer interprets, but comes up with something new on its own, gives itself a new text, then it ceases to be theology, as it is no longer interpreting but speaking in its own name.

Unity is rooted in faith, while theology is the domain of plurality, and in this respect, it is precisely adherence to the common reference point of faith that makes plurality in theology possible. Now, perhaps I have arrived at this claim somewhat quickly, so we should conclude by looking at both sides of the matter in a bit more detail.

We have, on the one hand, established that definiteness regarding its contents is an integral part of faith and that such definiteness likewise necessitates a competent authority. From this, we drew the conclusion that the Church, as the Church, cannot be without a voice but must have the gift of speech; that is, she must state what is essential to her. And this brings us to a crucial aspect of the act of faith. The faith of the Church does not exist as an ensemble of texts; rather, the texts, the words, exist because there is a corresponding subject in which the texts are grounded and by which they derive their inner coherence. Historically, the preaching of the Apostles gave rise to the social entity "Church" as a kind of historical subject. One becomes a believer by joining this communion of tradition, thought, and life; by beholding the living continuity of this communion throughout history; and then also by receiving a share of its way of understanding, of speaking, and of thinking. For the believer, however, this is not only some sociological subject, but a genuinely new subject called into being by the Holy Spirit, which for this very reason tears down the insurmountable barriers of human subjectivity and places man in contact with the fundamental basis of reality itself. By its very nature, faith always means believing *with* the whole

Church. The "I believe" of the Creed is not an isolated, private "I", but the common "I" of the Church. Faith becomes possible to the extent that *I* become one with this common "I", which does not nullify my own "I" but, rather, broadens it outward and in this way brings it completely to itself for the first time.

This is important because it leads us now into a realm that exists prior to language, thus also affirming, as it were, the theories regarding ever-new linguistic expression that I described earlier and, thus, also allowing us to get to the point of pluralism. The human words in which faith is expressed never wholly capture their content, which reaches into eternity. This is actually the kernel of truth at the core of those theories, which, in their worst form, amount to a Hinduization of the faith. The language of faith is not a mathematical language, the only language that is universal and unambiguous. The more deeply human words penetrate into the essence of reality, the more insufficient they become. All of this becomes even clearer if we turn our attention to the concrete testimony provided by the language of faith, characterized as it is by two immediately obvious facts: First, in many cases, it is a language of images, not a language of concepts, and, secondly, it presents itself in a historic succession of statements, in which the fundamental tension between the Old and the New Testament already demonstrates the extent to which the truth of the faith becomes accessible in language only within the inner coherence of the whole and not in isolated forms. If one eliminates the continuity of a subject that passes organically through all of history—a subject that, even though it experiences transformation, remains one with itself—then all that will remain are contradictory fragments of language that cannot be placed in any coherent sequence. The tendency to choose, what Church history would call "heresy", is a natural result of this; and so is the other tendency, to fall back on archaeology and to accept only certain parts as valid, the ones held to be most ancient. But as I have already said, such a reconstructed Christianity cannot help but be a selective Christianity, in which the tensions and the richness of the whole are lost. The intrinsic plurality of the symphony of faith is replaced by the disjointed pluralism of a selective Christianity characterized by subjectivity.

Moreover, we would also have to say that a disintegrative kind of pluralism arises where people are no longer up to the task of facing the great inner tension inherent in the wholeness of the faith. This always presupposes a prior narrowing and impoverishment that is not reversed by the proliferation of juxtaposed partial Christianities rising and falling one after another. On the contrary, all this does is bring fully to light the poverty of every solitary attempt. In the face of this pluralism of disintegration, which essentially consists of several different short-lived partial Christianities facing each other without communicating, there is fruitful theological pluralism where it is possible to relate the multiplicity of forms taken by historical manifestations of the faith to unity, a unity that, rather than extinguishing this multiplicity, recognizes it as the organic structure of truth that transcends man. Today, however, there is a suspicion, even among wholly church-minded theologians, that orthodox theology is hopelessly condemned to merely regurgitating official doctrinal statements and time-honored formulas. For the time being, the space for thought appears to be piled high with such a clutter of old and new decisions that one cannot avoid bumping into something at every step and there is simply no air to breathe freely. In order to get creative, to do something fruitful, it seems almost imperative to throw out the old dead wood and boldly move on, even to the point of open dissent. At this point, I think it would be helpful to take a quick glance at the natural sciences. They achieved their great successes, not through a free-floating creativity, but by strict adherence to their object. Of course, they must constantly approach this object again with new anticipatory hypotheses, search for new ways to probe it with questions, and make it give answers. But none of the answers, once given, can simply be discarded; on the contrary, the more numerous the answers become, the more possibilities for asking new questions open up and more concrete space is gained for real creativity, which no longer forges ahead into the void, but is capable of relating existing paths to one another and opening up new ones from there, thus also providing new contexts for, and thus new meanings to, what has been found so far without throwing it away. I believe that this is ultimately quite the same in theology. It is precisely the profusion of the forms taken by the faith in the unity of the Old and New Testament, of Scripture and the dogma of the ancient Church, of all of these elements together and of the ongoing life and faith of the Church that allows the questioning to become ever more exciting and mature because it presents itself in ever more diverse perspectives. Thus, it is still exciting to seek inner unity and the wholeness of truth in the grand historical structure of the faith, with all of its abundant contrasts.

# Index

faith and, 154–57
"Hinduization of Christianity" and, 162–67
history of idea of, 141–44
philosophy and, 147–49
social action and, 154–57
theology and, 149–53
truth and, 147–49
uniformity of man and, 144–47
polytheism, 18–19
positivism, 21
postexilic texts, 27
preexilic texts, 26–27
presentation, content and, 18, 20
Priestly Text (Genesis 1), 27, 62. *See also* Genesis, Book of
primacy of pope, 157–62
prophets of Israel, 28, 56, 94
Protestant theology, 52, 125–26, 128, 137–38
Psalms, 27, 31

Rad, Gerhard von, 25
Ratzinger, Joseph Cardinal. *See* Benedict XVI
reason
in creation, 41–46
creation and, 36–37, 39–41
cultic worship and, 48–54
demythologization of world and, 57–64
enlightenment and, 20
number usage, 46–48
promises of, 72–73
Reason of God, 18, 30–31, 36–37, 43–46
Sabbath and, 54–57
truth and, 46–48

redemption
about, 87–88
relationality of creation and, 104–8
relationality of creation
redemption and, 104–8
unity of mankind and, 70
repenting, 88–90
rest of God, 52, 54, 56
rhythm of creation, 46–48, 49, 56, 58, 62
Roman law, 131–32
Romans, 8, 63

Sabbath
Bloch on, 61–62
in creation account, 54–57
creation and, 48–49, 52–53
Torah and, 53
sacraments, 116–17, 121, 123, 127–28, 132, 136
salvation, 10, 15, 25, 63, 102, 104, 133, 139
Sartre, Jean-Paul, 66
Schmaus, Michael, 17
Schmitt, Carl, 144
Schneider, Reinhold, 19
scientific knowledge. *See also* technology
Bible and, 17–18
creation and evolution, 77–78
nature of, 51
science/sacred text dichotomy, 17, 20–23, 22–23
Scripture. *See also* New Testament; Old Testament
as "allegory," 36
creation theme in, 32–36